Robinson Crusoe and The Pirates

A Pantomime

Paul Reakes

A SAMUEL FRENCH ACTING EDITION

FOUNDED 1830

SAMUELFRENCH-LONDON.CO.UK
SAMUELFRENCH.COM

Copyright © 2000 by Paul Reakes
All Rights Reserved

ROBINSON CRUSOE AND THE PIRATES is fully protected under the copyright laws of the British Commonwealth, including Canada, the United States of America, and all other countries of the Copyright Union. All rights, including professional and amateur stage productions, recitation, lecturing, public reading, motion picture, radio broadcasting, television and the rights of translation into foreign languages are strictly reserved.

ISBN 978-0-573-16443-9

www.samuelfrench-london.co.uk

www.samuelfrench.com

FOR AMATEUR PRODUCTION ENQUIRIES

UNITED KINGDOM AND WORLD
EXCLUDING NORTH AMERICA
plays@SamuelFrench-London.co.uk
020 7255 4302/01

Each title is subject to availability from Samuel French,
depending upon country of performance.

CAUTION: Professional and amateur producers are hereby warned that *ROBINSON CRUSOE AND THE PIRATES* is subject to a licensing fee. Publication of this play does not imply availability for performance. Both amateurs and professionals considering a production are strongly advised to apply to the appropriate agent before starting rehearsals, advertising, or booking a theatre. A licensing fee must be paid whether the title is presented for charity or gain and whether or not admission is charged.

The professional rights in this play are controlled by Samuel French Ltd, 52 Fitzroy Street, London, W1T 5JR.

No one shall make any changes in this title for the purpose of production. No part of this book may be reproduced, stored in a retrieval system, or transmitted in any form, by any means, now known or yet to be invented, including mechanical, electronic, photocopying, recording, videotaping, or otherwise, without the prior written permission of the publisher. No one shall upload this title, or part of this title, to any social media websites.

The right of Paul Reakes to be identified as author of this work has been asserted by him in accordance with Section 77 of the Copyright, Designs and Patents Act 1988

CHARACTERS

Robinson Crusoe
Ma Crusoe, his mother
Willy Crusoe, his brother
Polly Perkins
Captain Bowsprit
Bessie Bowsprit, his daughter
Blackbeard, the infamous pirate
Patch, his henchman
The Crimson Hawk, a female pirate
Man Friday
King Neptune
The Medicine Man
A Gorilla

Chorus of: Townsfolk, Sailors, Pirates, Undersea Life, Islanders, Island Wildlife

MUSICAL NUMBERS

ACT I

1	**Song and Dance**	Polly, Chorus and Dancers
2	**Romantic Duet**	Robinson and Polly
3	**Comedy Song and Dance**	Ma, Willy, and Chorus
4	**Song and Dance**	Principals and Chorus
5	**Comedy Duet**	Willy and Bessie
6	**Comedy Song and Dance**	Ma, Willy, Bessie, Robinson and Chorus
7	**Undersea Dance**	Chorus, Dancers and Children
8	**Song and Dance**	Robinson, Neptune and Chorus

ACT II

9	**Song and Dance**	Chorus and Dancers
10	**Comedy Song and Dance**	Ma, Willy, Bessie and Dancers
11	**Wildlife Dance**	Dancers and Children
12	**Romantic Solo**	Robinson
13	**Duet and Dance**	Robinson and Friday
14	**Dance**	Chorus or Speciality Dancer/s
15	**Song and Dance** (optional)	Principals, Chorus and Gorilla
16	**House Song**	Ma, Willy and audience
17	**Finale Song or a Reprise**	All

Choice of songs is at the discretion of the Director, but please read the note supplied by the Performing Right Society on page vi carefully.

SYNOPSIS OF SCENES

ACT I

SCENE 1 Quayside at Bobbin-on-the-Briny

SCENE 2 Below Decks

SCENE 3 Deck of *The Dancing Dolphin*

SCENE 4 Adrift at Sea

SCENE 5 Neptune's Palace Under the Sea

ACT II

SCENE 1 The Desert Island

SCENE 2 Another Part of the Island

SCENE 3 Robinson's Hut

SCENE 4 Another Part of the Island

SCENE 5 The Temple of Boogar

SCENE 6 Before the Voyage Home

SCENE 7 The Grand Finale

CHARACTERS AND COSTUMES

Robinson Crusoe (Principal Boy) is a handsome, fearless young chap with a winning smile and a smashing pair of legs! He is the sensible member of the crazy Crusoe family. A charismatic personality is needed with a strong singing voice and dancing ability. Apart from his everyday clothes, he gets to wear a nautical outfit and a natty costume made from natural materials. Magnificent Finale costume.

Ma Crusoe (Dame) is his widowed mother. She is loud, lumpy and ludicrous, but you can't help liking the old girl. She enjoys both fun and misery. She is always on friendly and confidential terms with the audience and never misses an opportunity of involving them. As well as her everyday costume, she gets to wear some outrageous nautical outfits in varying stages of disarray after the shipwreck. Special Finale costume.

Willy Crusoe is Robinson's dopey brother. His childish vulnerability makes him an instant favourite with the audience, especially the youngsters. He is involved in plenty of audience participation and buffoonery. Singing and dancing ability an advantage. Comical costumes, including baggy bermuda shorts and nautical outfit for the sea voyage. Finale costume.

Polly Perkins/The Crimson Hawk. These are two very different characters played by the same actress. A versatile and competent player is needed. When Polly drops her disguise it must come as a big surprise, not only to the other characters, but to the audience as well. In the programme use the actress's real name for Polly and a pseudonym for the Crimson Hawk. **Polly Perkins** is a pretty and petite barmaid. Her voice is soft, and her manner is gentle and unassuming. A pleasant singing voice and dancing ability. The traditional principal girl, in fact! Neat, picturesque barmaid's costume with mob cap and apron, etc. **The Crimson Hawk** is the complete opposite! She is a tall, swaggering swashbuckler, with a no-nonsense voice and commanding presence. Although a pirate, she is a humane one, and must be likeable. A kind of female Errol Flynn! Her all-crimson costume consists of: bolero or jerkin, wide-sleeved blouse, sash and tights. A wide-brimmed hat with tall crimson feather, and high-heeled thigh boots will give her extra height. Her hair is concealed by a crimson bandanna and the upper part of her face is covered by a crimson mask. Magnificent Finale costume.

Captain Bowsprit is a gruff old mariner who doesn't suffer fools gladly. His speech is clipped, more used to barking out orders than social chit chat. He is fearless and unafraid, even when threatened by the evil Blackbeard. He looks very smart in his blue sea captain's uniform with tricorn hat, brass buttons and white breeches and stockings.

Bessie Bowsprit is the Captain's daughter and Willy's girlfriend. She is a fluffy, empty-headed young woman with affected speech and manner. She and dozy Willy are well suited! She also gets to cry and scream a lot. Singing and dancing ability an advantage. All her costumes are fussy and frilly, including her nautical outfits. Finale costume.

Blackbeard, the infamous pirate, is a big, black-hearted villain with a big black beard to match. He hails from the West Country, and specializes in growls, snarls and plenty of "ha hars!" He never misses an opportunity of stirring the audience up into a frenzy of boos and hisses. A thoroughly nasty piece of work! Traditional pirate captain's outfit with red coat, sea boots and tricorn hat.

Patch is his long-suffering henchman. He is a lovable rogue rather than an out-and-out nasty. The audience should take a liking to him, despite his associations with Blackbeard. He is a roly-poly little man with a few missing teeth and a patch over one eye. Traditional pirate costume with voluminous coat, striped jersey and bandana.

Man Friday is a young native of the island. At first he is afraid and nervous of the alien Robinson, but once the language barrier is broken down, he loses his timidity and they become good friends. Singing and dancing ability an advantage. He only appears in Act II.

King Neptune is ruler of the undersea world. A grand old man, made grumpy by a persistent head cold. This has given him a red nose which shines out from his flowing white hair and beard. He wears a crown and regal robes of aquatic design, decorated with glittering shells and scales, etc. He only appears in Act I, and could double with——

The Medicine Man. A terrifying and menacing figure. He must be agile, his movements varying from snake-like slithers to leopard-like leaps. His voice too changes from a deep growl to a high-pitched whine. His make-up and costume should be grotesque and frightening. He only appears in Act II.

A Gorilla, who provides plenty of comic monkey business. He also gets involved in some of the dancing and chase scenes. For the chase scene he wears running shorts and a number. Perhaps a glittery top hat and bow tie for the Finale. He only appears in Act II.

The Chorus, **Dancers** and **Children** have plenty to do, appearing as Townsfolk, Sailors, Pirates, Undersea life, Islanders, and Island Wildlife. All participate in the action and musical numbers.

P.R.

PRODUCTION NOTES

STAGING

The pantomime offers opportunities for elaborate staging, but can be produced quite simply if facilities and funds are limited. There are five full sets: Quayside at Bobbin-on-the-Briny, Deck of *The Dancing Dolphin*, Neptune's Palace Under the Sea, The Desert Island, and The Temple of Boogar. (This last scene can be played to the Desert Island setting with the addition of the idol and altar). All these scenes are interlinked with tabs or frontcloth scenes. The last set can be used for the Finale with the removal of the idol and altar.

THE CRIMSON HAWK'S SHIP

This is a painted cut-out representing masts and sails seen at a distance. It is fixed to a small trolley and pulled on and off behind the bulwarks. If there is a problem hoisting the Jolly Roger, the "ship" can sail into view with the flag already flying.

THE SHARK

This works on the same principle as the ship. A large shark's fin cut-out fixed to a trolley and operated between the wave ground row and bath tub.

THE SEA SERPENT

It can be played by members of the chorus in a serpent body and head, or, a well constructed (perhaps animated?) life-size model could be used.

ROBINSON'S HUT

This is just a three-sided screen. It has a practical opening at the front, covered by a skin. It is painted to represent a crude bamboo structure with large leaves forming the roof.

THE IDOL AND ALTAR

The Idol must be big enough to dominate the back of the stage. It should be hideous to behold—half man, half demon, with one enormous eye, horns and a huge, fang-filled mouth. Whether it is constructed three dimensional, or as a flat cut-out, is left to the expertise of your scenic design crew. Robinson must be able to stand inside or behind it without being seen but he must also have visibility. The idol's arms and claws are hollow and flexible and camouflaged to blend with the rest of the body. Robinson simply wears them like the sleeves of a coat with gloves attached. The arms must remain perfectly still until indicated in the script. The most comfortable static position to maintain is left to the performer. An amplification system is concealed in the idol for when it roars and Robinson speaks. (The deep, unearthly roars could be done from an offstage microphone.) **The altar** should look as if it's been carved from stone. It needs to be strong, as Ma Crusoe has to lie on it! Also, it has to be big enough to house Man Friday and the treasure chest. Its lid slides open. It is advisable to have these two pieces of scenery well in use before the actual performance.

P.R.

Other pantomimes by Paul Reakes published by
Samuel French Ltd:

Babes in the Wood
Dick Turpin
King Arthur,
a pantomime adventure in Camelot
Little Jack Horner
Little Miss Muffet
Old Mother Hubbard
Santa in Space
Sinbad the Sailor

ACT I

Scene 1

The quayside at Bobbin-in-the-Briny

The prow and figurehead of The Dancing Dolphin *is* UR. *A gangplank leads down from the deck.* UL *is part of the harbour wall with ropes, barrels, etc.* L *is the* Sea Dog Inn *with practical front door and hanging signboard. A small table and a couple of stools are set outside the Inn. The side wings represent typical quayside buildings. The backcloth shows sea, sky and the rest of the harbour*

When the CURTAIN *rises, Polly Perkins and Chorus, as Townsfolk and Sailors, are discovered. They go straight into the opening song and dance*

Song 1

After the number, the Chorus exit in various directions

Polly goes into the Inn

Patch creeps on from behind the Inn

He looks cautiously about, then beckons to someone

Villainous music and Blackbeard enters

They move DS

Patch (*obviously pleased with his surroundings*) Well, this looks like a nice little spot, don't it, Cap'n?
Blackbeard (*scowling*) Sure you ain't got that patch over yer good eye!?
Patch I mean—compared that other place. That [nearby town or village]!
Blackbeard (*furiously grabbing Patch*) Belay! Never mention that rat 'ole again, Mr Patch, if you know what's good for ee!
Patch (*indicating the audience*) The natives seem friendly enough!
Blackbeard (*scanning the audience and growling*) Gerr! Another crew of

scurvy, lily-livered swabs by the look of 'em! (*He stirs the audience up*) What are ya?!
Patch 'Ush, Cap'n. Tain't wise to go upsettin' 'em. You'm still in 'idin', don't forget!
Blackbeard (*grabbing Patch, roaring*) Forget! Forget! 'Ow *can* I forget! (*He releases Patch*) Me, the Mighty Blackbeard, scourge o' the Seven Seas, forced to lie low on dry land wi'out a ship or crew! 'Tis enough to make a man walk 'is own plank! (*With smouldering venom*) An' all the time I be dry docked 'ere, that swab be out plunderin' the 'igh seas—*My* seas!
Patch You mean—The Crimson 'Awk, Cap'n?
Blackbeard (*turning with a roar*) Arr! The Crimson Hawk! (*He spits*) Devil rot 'im.
Patch (*nervously*) 'Tis... 'Tis even worse than you think, Cap'n.
Blackbeard (*rounding on him*) What do ee mean?!
Patch (*cowering*) I... I don't know if I should tell ee, Cap'n...
Blackbeard (*grabbing Patch; roaring*) Tell me, or I'll rip out yer innards an' use 'em fer braces!
Patch (*gulping*) T-tis about the Crimson 'Awk... E ain't a 'e... 'E's a (*he gulps*) she!
Blackbeard (*releasing Patch and staggering back, aghast*) What!! The Crimson 'Awk—*a woman*!!
Patch S-so I've 'eard, Cap'n.
Blackbeard (*exploding*) Agghr! Blisterin' barnacles an' boilin' buckets o' blood!! The Great Blackbeard outdone by a petticoat! I'll be the laughin' stock of the pirates' union! I've go to get back to sea an' scupper this female! (*He moves* DR)

Polly comes out of the Inn and goes to tidy the stools and wipe the table top

Patch (*seeing her*) Look, Cap'n, look! There be somethin' to cheer ee up.
Blackbeard (*looking and liking what he sees*) Arr! She be a trim little craft, she be. I likes the cut of er jib.

With her back to them, Polly leans across to wipe the table top. Both men watch her bobbing bottom

Patch (*with a nudge*) A nice little stern on er, eh, Cap'n?
Blackbeard I reckon I'll be goin' along side! (*He adjusts his hat and swaggers over to Polly*)

Patch follows him

Top o' the mornin', missy!

Act I, Scene 1

Polly straightens up and is surprised to see them standing so close

Polly Oh! Good morning, gentlemen.
Blackbeard (*leering at her*) An' what might your name be?
Polly (*with a bob*) Polly Perkins, sir. I'm the barmaid. Can I get anything for you? A tankard of ale? A tot of rum? Something to eat?
Blackbeard Later per'aps, but first—I'll be 'aving a kiss!
Polly (*good-humouredly*) I'm afraid that's not on the menu, sir.
Blackbeard 'Tis now! Come 'ere! (*He grabs Polly and tries to kiss her*)
Polly (*struggling and calling out*) Let go! Let go of me! Stop that! Let go!

Robinson Crusoe, young and handsome, enters from R

Robinson Hey! What's going on? Leave that girl alone!

Robinson rushes across and hauls Blackbeard away from Polly

Blackbeard Eh...! What the... (*He looks Robinson up and down, then snarls*) An' who, by thunder, might you be?
Robinson My name is Robinson Crusoe. That young lady is a friend of mine.
Blackbeard So what! There be plenty to go round, I reckon! (*He advances on Polly*)
Robinson (*seizing his arm and swinging him around*) I'm warning you! Lay a finger on her again and I'll prune that overgrown hedge of yours! (*He flicks Blackbeard's beard*)
Blackbeard (*exploding*) Gerr! Boilin' buckets o' blood!! Do ee know who you'm atalkin' to?!
Robinson (*calmly*) No, but I'm sure I've seen you on *Animal Hospital*.

With a roar, Blackbeard advance on Robinson. Patch quickly gets between them

Patch I reckon we'd better be goin' now! (*Aside to Blackbeard*) Don't draw attention to yerself, Cap'n! (*Aloud*) Let's go and look at the [local place of interest].

Blackbeard glares at Robinson, then allows Patch to lead him to the DL *exit. He turns for a parting shot*

Blackbeard Don't think you've 'eard the last o' this, you scurvy land lubber! (*To the audience*) An' that goes fer you lot an' all!

He engages in byplay with the audience until Patch finally succeeds in dragging him out DL

Polly (*to Robinson with an exaggerated curtsy*) Thank you for coming to my rescue, kind sir.
Robinson (*with an exaggerated bow*) Pray don't mention it, dear lady.

They both laugh. Polly goes back to wiping the table. Slight pause

Er... Polly?
Polly Yes, Rob?
Robinson (*moving to her*) How's your grandmother?
Polly Grandmother? Oh, she's quite well at the moment, thank you. Why do you ask?
Robinson Well, the last three times I asked you to go out with me she was suddenly taken ill and you had to rush to her sickbed. And each time you stayed away for months.
Polly I know, Rob. I'm sorry. But I am her only living relative. I can't leave the poor old dear alone when she's ill, can I?
Robinson (*moving away*) I was beginning to think that you don't want to go out with me.
Polly (*moving to him, smiling*) Why don't you try asking me again?
Robinson (*turning to her*) All right! Polly, will you go out with me?
Polly Of course I will. When?
Robinson Tonight?
Polly I'd love to.
Robinson (*taking her hands, overjoyed*) Brilliant! (*He shuts his eyes tight and mumbles to himself*)
Polly What on earth are you doing?
Robinson (*still with eyes shut*) I'm praying your granny doesn't have a relapse.
Polly (*smiling*) Say one for me while you're at it.

Song 2

Romantic duet and dance. After the number, Robinson walks Polly to the Inn door

Robinson Until tonight, then.
Polly Until tonight. (*She kisses his cheek*)

Polly goes into the Inn

Robinson (*stroking his cheek*) Cor! (*He shuts his eyes*) Keep on taking the tablets, Granny!
Ma (*off R, calling*) Willy! Willy Crusoe! Where are ya?! Willy!
Robinson That sounds like Ma! I wonder what's up!

Act I, Scene 1   5

Ma Crusoe bustles on from R

Ma (*calling*) Willy! Has anyone seen my Willy?! (*She spots Robinson*) Ah! Robbie! 'Ave you seen your brother Willy?
Robinson Not since I left the house, Ma. Why? What's he done?
Ma It's not *what* 'e's done, it's what 'e *might* do! Oo! I'm that worried about 'im I don't know whether I'm on me base or me apex! I'm scared stiff 'e might *do* somethin'!
Robinson (*laughing*) Well, he never has, so why should he start now?
Ma Robinson Crusoe! Don't talk about yer brother like that! You know 'e's delicate. It's not 'is fault! 'E takes after me! An' I'm very delicate in case you 'adn't noticed!
Robinson But what's wrong with him?
Ma Well, 'e's... (*She is suddenly conscious of the audience*) It's a family matter. It's private. I can't discuss it in front of all these people. Who are they anyway, Robbie? What are they doin' 'ere? Is it the [local reference]?
Robinson I don't think so, Ma. They seem like a nice friendly bunch.
Ma Do they? (*To the audience*) *Are* you a nice friendly bunch?

"Yes!" from the audience

(*To Robinson*) Oh, I'm not so sure! (*She points someone out*) Look at 'im there! 'E looks like 'e could chew iron bars an' spit out nails! (*She points to someone else*) An' look at 'er! I'm sure she's the one who pushed in front of me at [local store]! An' look at that little one! 'E'd scare the pants off Godzilla! (*Or she does a topical gag*)
Robinson I'm sure they're OK, Ma. Why don't you introduce yourself?
Ma Oh, tell 'em who hi ham, y' mean! Well, I'll 'ave a go! But the moment they start to turn ugly—correction—ugli*er*, you call [local police]. 'Ere goes! (*To the audience*) Hallo!

The audience call back

(*To Robinson*) So far, so good! (*To the audience*) I am Ma Crusoe. A poor widow. (*She encourages "Ahh's" from the audience*) I've got two sons, Willy and Robinson. This is Robinson. I called him that because 'e's got lots of bottle. 'E's a fine lookin' lad, isn't 'e? (*Confidentially*) 'E gets some funny looks, though. I can't understand it. It must be the way 'e parts 'is 'air. (*To Robinson*) You're right. They don't seem a bad lot, after all.
Robinson So, what's wrong with Willy?
Ma Y'know 'e's been courtin' Bessie Bowsprit for years an' years—ever since Coronation Street was just a footpath—well, this mornin' 'e 'eard she was seen out last night with another fella! One of them posh blokes from

up [local "posh" area]! The poor lamb's broken-'earted! 'E might try an' do 'imself a mischief! Ooo!

Robinson Don't worry, Ma. Willy won't do anything like that. He hasn't got the energy.

Ma But 'e was so upset! 'E was in a turmoil! I've never seen 'is tur so moiled! (*She moves* R. *Melodramatically*) Oh, my poor child! My poor, poor child! Where can he be?! Oh, where can my little Willy be! (*She leans tragically against the proscenium arch*)

Robinson (*looking off* L) There's no need to go for an Oscar, Ma. Here he comes now.

Willy Crusoe enters from DL

He just stands there, a forlorn, dejected figure

Willy (*without expression*) 'Ullo, Ma. 'Ullo, Robbie.

Ma (*rushing over to him*) Willy! My little sugar plum! Come to Mummy! Come to Mummy!

Comic business as Willy starts to cry and wails loudly. Ma hugs him to her bosom

There, there! Oh, diddums. Mummy make it better. (*She gives him her apron to cry into*)

Comic business

You've 'ad me witless with worry. Where 'ave you been? What 'ave you been doin'?

Willy I... I... (*He dissolves into tears and wails again, grabbing at Ma's skirts*)

Ma Oh, what am I goin' to do! The poor lad's unconsociable!

Robinson (*taking charge*) Let me deal with this. (*He gets between them and disentangles Willy from Ma's skirts*) Now, stop blubbering, Willy, and listen to me. Do you love Bessie Bowsprit?

Willy Yes!

Robinson There's only one thing to be done. You must ask Bessie to marry you.

Willy is dumbstruck and just stands there with his mouth gaping open

Ma 'Ere! That'd be nice! 'Er father, Captain Bowsprit, owns 'is own ship! (*To the audience*) 'E's got the biggest windjammer you ever saw!

Robinson What do you say, Willy?

They look at him. He remains transfixed with his mouth open

Ma I think 'e's gone into postnasal shock! Oh, do somethin', Robbie, before people start postin' letters in 'is mouth!
Robinson (*snapping his fingers in front of Willy's face*) Willy!
Willy (*lurching back into life*) A-ask B-B-Bessie to m-marry me! (*He panics*) I can't... I couldn't... I'm scared!!
Robinson There's nothing to be scared about. You just say to her—(*he gets down on one knee*) "Bessie, will you marry me?"(*He stands*) It's simple. You do *want* to marry her, don't you?
Willy (*all soppy*) Oh, yes... I love her. (*Timid again*) You ask her for me, Robbie.
Robinson I can't. It's got to come from you. I know it's difficult, but you've got to try and act like a man.
Ma (*aside to the audience with a wink*) An' 'e should know!
Willy (*standing to attention*) All right! I'll do it!
Robinson Attaboy!
Willy (*wilting again*) Next week!
Robinson You'll do it straight away before she gets too interested in that other chap.
Ma (*looking off* R) Hey! Bessie's comin' up the street!
Willy Ooow!! (*He makes for the exit* DL)
Robinson (*grabbing him and pulling him back*) You can do it. I know you can.

Willy shakes with fright. Robinson positions him C *and tidies him up*

Come on, Ma. (*He moves to the exit* DL) Let's leave him to it.
Ma (*going to Willy*) Be brave, my little soldier. (*She kisses his cheek*) And if she gets rough—call for Mummy. (*She joins Robinson*) And remember—faint heart never won a pig in a poke!

Tearfully, Ma exit DL

Robinson gives Willy the thumbs up sign and follows Ma out

Left alone, Willy's nerve cracks and he is about to run off L, *when Bessie Bowsprit enters from* R

Bessie Hallo, Willy!
Willy Oh! Bello Hessie! I mean—Hallo Bessie.
Bessie (*moving* C) What are you doing?
Willy Nothin'.

Bessie Neither am I. (*She giggles and moves over to him*) Do you fancy doing something—together. (*She moves in close*)
Willy Like what?
Bessie Let's go for a walk— (*she moves in very close*) up Lovers' Lane.

Willy ducks away C, *causing Bessie to almost topple over*

Willy (*sulkily*) Wouldn't you rather go with that other chap? The one you was out with last night.
Bessie (*moving to him*) I'd rather go with you, Willy.
Willy (*turning his back on her*) Humph! So you say!
Bessie I only went out with him because Daddy said I had to. Oh, Willy, it's you I want to be with. Really I do. I… (*All soppy*) I love you.
Willy (*facing her, overjoyed*) An' I love you!
Bessie Oh, Willy!
Willy Oh, Bessie!

They do a soppy embrace

Bessie, there's somethin' I want to ask you…
Bessie What is it?
Willy Bessie, will you… Oh!

Comic business as he gets down on one knee and faces the wrong way

Bessie, will… Where've you gone? (*He wriggles around to face her*) Bessie, will…

Captain Bowsprit enters on the deck of the ship, UR

Captain (*barking*) Ahoy there!

Startled, Willy falls flat on his face. The Captain comes down the gangplank

Bessie Hallo, Daddy.

The Captain looks down at Willy, who rolls onto his back, feet in the air, and gives a wave. He clambers to his feet, using the rigid Captain as a support. Comic business as he straightens the Captain's uniform and polishes his buttons, etc. He gives a stupid salute

Captain (*to the audience*) Fella's an idiot! (*He goes to Bessie*) Well, m'dear. Enjoy your evenin' out with young Fullbanks at [local "posh" area]?
Bessie No, Daddy.

Act I, Scene 1

Captain What! Oh, well, no matter. Plenty more fish in the sea. Take yer time, m'girl. Important to find the right man. Someone who can handle his tiller and navigate yer passage. Can't have you marryin' a milksop!

Willy hops about and waves his hand trying to attract the Captain's attention

Willy Er ... Er ... Er...
Captain (*looking at Willy, then back to Bessie*) What's the matter with the fella?
Bessie Just before you came along he was going to ask me something.
Captain (*getting enraged*) Was he, by thunder!

Bellowing, he forces Willy back against the proscenium arch R. *During the following tirade, Willy slides down the proscenium arch. He ends up sitting on the ground, a gibbering wreck*

Well! What was it?! Out with it! Speak up! Speak up! Out with it! Speak up! Out with it! (*To the audience*) Fella's a complete nincompoop! (*He moves to Bessie*)
Willy (*standing up with a desperate cry*) I was gonna ask her to marry me!
Captain (*bellowing*) What!!
Bessie (*ecstatically*) Oh, Willy!

The Captain strides back to Willy, who flattens himself against the proscenium arch again

Captain (*roaring*) Ask her to marry *you*! Who are ya?! What are ya?! Got any money?
Willy (*sliding down the arch, a squeak*) No!
Captain Then you ain't got my daughter!
Bessie (*rushing across*) But, Daddy—we love each other!
Captain Love! What the blazes has that got to do with gettin' married?! Want you spliced to someone with money and position, m'girl! (*He glares at Willy*) Not some penniless guttersnipe!
Bessie | (*together*) | But, Daddy...
Willy | | Captain, I...
Captain (*roaring*) Silence between decks! Wasted enough time here! (*To Bessie*) Let's be goin'! (*He strides up to the gangplank*)
Bessie (*going to Willy, tearfully*) Oh, Willy!
Captain (*barking*) Step lively, girl! That's an order!

Obediently, Bessie goes up the gangplank. She looks back at Willy, bursts into tears and rushes on to the ship to exit UR

Captain stomps up the gangplank and exits UR

Willy moves up to watch him go, then turns to face front, a picture of absolute dejection and misery

Ma Crusoe pokes her head out from behind the wall on R

Ma (*brightly*) Yoohoo! Is it safe to come in? (*She moves to Willy. Eagerly*) Well, Willy, 'ow did it go? When can we book [local church]?
Willy (*turning to her and starting to blub*) Oh, Ma!
Ma Oh, crikey!

Robinson enters DL, *with a letter*

Robinson Oh, dear! I take it Bessie said no.

The Chorus drift on from various directions

Polly enters from the Inn

Willy (*between sobs and sniffs*) She didn't get the chance. Her father came along an' spoilt everthin'! He said he'd never let his daughter marry a snuttergipe ... A gittertripe ... An idiot like me! (*He wails*)
Ma (*outraged*) Oh! What sauce! The toffee-nosed old twit... Wait till I see 'im! Upsettin' my little lambkins! (*She sees the letter*) What 'ave you got there, Robbie?
Robinson (*holding the letter up*) It's a letter, Ma.
Ma (*to the audience*) My kids are pure genius! (*To Robinson*) I can see it's a letter, you great big steamin' nit! Who's it from? What's it say?
Robinson (*opening the letter*) I don't know yet. The postman's only just given it to me. (*He looks at the letter*) It's from Loophole, Diddleum and Costplenty. Solicitors!
Ma Oh, no! What 'ave you been up to now!
Robinson (*reading*) "Dear Mr Robinson Crusoe. It is with deep regret that we have to inform you of the death of your Great Uncle, Rear Admiral Horatio Benbow, RN".
Ma Oh, poor old Horatio. Did 'e go down with 'is ship or was 'e in port at the time?
Robinson It doesn't say.
Ma Oh well, knowin' Horatio, I bet port 'ad somethin' to do with it. Go on! Go on!
Robinson (*reading*) "According to his last will and testament, you are his sole beneficiary"...
Ma Benny who?

Act I, Scene 1

Robinson Beneficiary. That means he left me everything!

All gasp

> (*Reading*) "If you will present yourself at our offices you will learn something to your advantage".
> **Ma** (*ecstatically*) We're rich!! We're rich!!

Ma dances about with Willy and Robinson, singing

> "We're in the money, we're in the money!" Well, don't just stand there, Robbie! Get down to thingamy's an' bring back all that lovely loot! (*She pushes him towards the exit* DL)
> **Robinson** (*laughing*) All right, Ma!

Robinson runs out DL

Ma (*to the Chorus*) Congratulate me, folks! The Crusoes are rich at last!

The Chorus come forward to congratulate Ma and Willy

> (*To the audience*) Goodbye poverty! Hallo luxury! It'll be soft paper in the loo an' real butter for tea from now on! I'll buy a house up [local expensive area]! I'll buy two! Blow it, I'll buy the whole street! (*She is serious for a moment*) But I won't let it change my life— (*she lets rip again*) not flippin' much I won't! Yipeee!

Song 3

A "money" oriented song for Ma, Willy, Polly and the Chorus

Willy (*after the song*) I'm gonna find Bessie an' 'er dad! He's bound to let us get married now our family's rich!

Willy runs up the gangplank and exits UR

Robinson enters DL, *dragging a sea chest*

Robinson Give me a hand someone.

One of the Chorus steps forward to help, but Ma pushes them back

Ma Out the way! That's our dosh! I'll man'andle it! (*She flexes her muscles*) They don't call me the Charlie Dimmock of [local place] for nothin'!

Ma and Robinson carry the chest C and put it down. The others gather around to look

Where's the rest?
Robinson That's all there is, Ma. One sea chest.
Ma (*disappointed*) Oh! (*She brightens*) Well, it weighs a ton. It must be full of gold! Open it! Open it! The suspenders is killin' me!

Robinson produces a key and kneels down to unlock the chest. All watch with eager anticipation. He slowly opens the lid, DS, facing the audience. All bend forward to look, then step back in amazement. The Chorus start to giggle. Ma and Robinson are gobsmacked

But ... But ... But ... Where's all the money?! Where's all the cash?! There's nothin' in here but *this*! (*She takes a variety of comically useless objects from the chest. Ad lib*) And *this*! And *this*! And *this*! Oh, Robinson! We've been diddled!
Robinson (*amused in spite of the situation*) It certainly looks that way, Ma.
Man (*to Ma, tongue in cheek*) So, it doesn't look like we'll be seeing you up [local expensive area] after all.

The others laugh

Ma (*fuming*) Oh, go and boil yer 'ead! Go away, the lot of ya!

Laughing, the Chorus exit in various directions

Ma slams down the lid of the chest and sits on it, sulking

Robinson Never mind, Ma. We're no worse off than we were before.
Ma Oh, that rotten old Horatio! If 'e wasn't already dead, I'd murder 'im!

Captain Bowsprit enters UR, and comes down the gangplank. He is followed by Willy and Bessie, holding hands and acting all soppy

Captain (*barking*) Ahoy there!
Ma (*to the audience*) Oh, that's all we need—Captain Pugwash! Oh, yes! (*She jumps up and goes to the Captain. Very indignantly*) I've got a bone to pick with you! How dare you incinerate our family's rubbish! What d'you mean by sayin' my Willy isn't good enough to marry your daughter——
Willy (*trying to intervene*) Ma——
Ma (*ranting on to Captain*) I'll 'ave you know, Popeye, we can trace our family back to Noah and 'is wife, Joan of Arc!

Act I, Scene 1   13

Willy Ma——
Ma There were Crusoes at the Battle of Agincourt when Christopher Columbus discovered Doctor Livingstone at the South Pole...
Willy (*loudly*) Ma! It's all right. Captain Bowsprit said I can marry Bessie.
Ma (*to Captain, shamefaced*) Did ya?
Captain I did. Tells me his family's come into money. Fella's a complete ignoramus, but I don't mind that as long as he's a rich one.
Ma Well, you can forget that—cos there's no money!
Captain ⎫
Willy   ⎬ (*together*) No money!!?
Bessie   ⎭
Ma Not a bent penny!
Willy But I thought Uncle Horatio left you everything, Robbie.
Robinson He did. And it's all in that chest.
Ma (*throwing open the chest lid*) And it's a load of old junk!
Robinson Sorry, Willy. We're just as poor as we ever were.
Captain In that case—the marriage is off! Come, Bessie! (*He heads for the gangplank*)
Ma (*stopping him*) Just a minute, 'Ornblower! You're one of them Jolly Jack Tars, aren't ya?
Captain I'm a naval man, if that's what you mean!
Ma (*eyeing his paunch*) Yes, I can see that. 'Ow would you like a nice chest to go with yer naval.
Captain (*shocked*) I beg your pardon!
Ma Not *this* chest, you mucky mariner, *that* one! (*She points to the sea chest*) It's no use to us. You might as well 'ave it—for a price!
Captain Don't need it. Already got one. (*He turns to go*)
Ma (*pulling him back*) Well, treat yourself to another one. You can keep yer spare anchor in it. Go on, give it the once over.

Reluctantly, the Captain inspects the chest. With his back to Ma, he bends over to look inside

Captain Mm! Looks a bit wonky an' worm-eaten!
Ma Yes! Especially from where I'm standin'! You can 'ave it for a fiver.
Captain No. Not interested. (*He spots something*) Hold hard! What's this? Something stuck down the side ... Piece of paper... (*He straightens up, holding a folded parchment*)

The others gather around

Robinson What is it?
Ma Probably Uncle Horatio's bill from Oddbins!

Captain (*opening the parchment*) By thunder! By thunder!
Ma Never mind the weather forecast—what is it?
Captain It's a map of an island! With all the latitudes and longitudes of how to find it!
Ma (*snatching the parchment*) Let's 'ave a butchers! Oh, so it is! Looks like someone's been playin' noughts and crosses on it. There's some writin'... (*She peers and reads*) "bulk—of—treasure—buried—here". (*She looks up, puzzled*) Wos that mean—bulk of treasure... (*She suddenly realizes*) It's a treasure map! We've found a treasure map!! A treasure map!! (*She gets very excited*)

The others try to calm her down

During this, Blackbeard and Patch poke their heads out from behind the wall L and listen

Robinson Steady, Ma, steady! Calm down!
Ma (*waving the map*) But it's a measure trap! I mean, a treasure map! We've found a treasure map!
Robinson Let me see. (*He takes the parchment*) There's a name scrawled at the bottom. (*He reads*) "Property of Captain J Flint".
Captain Flint!
Robinson Have you heard of him, Captain?
Captain Heard of him! What sailor hasn't? Flint was a notorious pirate. Plundered thousands of ships in his day. Dead now. But his treasure was never recovered. Must have buried it on that island. It's got to be worth millions! Millions!
Ma (*getting worked up again*) Millions! We're gonna be millionaires!! We're gonna be millionaires!! (*To the audience*) An' I didn't even 'ave to ring a friend!! (*She gets very excited again*)

The others try to calm her down

Blackbeard and Patch withdraw their heads

Willy What are we gonna do?
Robinson Well, as Uncle Horatio left me the map, I suppose it's my duty to find the treasure and dig it up.
Ma There's no suppose about it! An' I'll 'elp ya! (*To Willy*) Quick! Run down to [local shop] an' buy a spade!
Robinson Not so fast, Ma. First we've got to find the island. And for that we'll need a ship.

A moment of despair

Act I, Scene 1   15

Bessie Daddy—*you've* got a ship.
Others (*looking at Captain*) Oh, yes!
Captain Out of the question!
Ma Oh, go on! Let us use your ship. We'll let you drive.
Captain Impossible!
Robinson (*businesslike*) Captain Bowsprit, I am prepared to pay you handsomely for the hire of your vessel.
Captain Pay me? What with?
Robinson A share of the treasure. What do you say, Captain? (*He holds out the map to him*) Is it a bargain?
Captain Well... Ay! 'Tis a bargain! (*He takes the map and shakes Robinson's hand*)

The others cheer

(*Bellowing*) Silence between decks!!

They go silent

First I want to lay down me articles.
Ma (*shocked*) What, in the street?!
Captain Once we put to sea, my word is law. Understand!
Others (*saluting*) Ay, ay, Captain!
Captain No-one must know that we're goin' after treasure. Absolute secrecy! Understand!
Others (*saluting in a whisper*) Ay, ay, Captain.
Robinson When do we leave?
Captain No point in dallyin'. We set sail on the next tide!

The others cheer

Ma (*saluting and doing a "Robert Newton"*) Ay, ay, Cap'n! Yo heave ho an' a bottle of brown! Ha har! Jim lad! Pieces o' eight! Pieces o' eight! Ha har! (*She hops about on one leg, etc.*)
Captain (*giving her a look*) Ye-es... (*To the audience*) Wonder if I'm doin' the right thing! (*To all*) Make ready! Jump to it! I'll give orders for sailin'!

Captain goes up the gangplank and exits UR

Robinson We'd better hurry and pack. There isn't much time.

Ma, Willy and Bessie exit R, *removing the sea chest*

(*Turning to Polly*) Well, this a turn up. I didn't have a sea voyage in mind when I asked you out tonight.

Polly You ... You mean you want me to go with you?
Robinson Of course.
Polly But I'm not family.
Robinson No—(*he takes her hands*) not yet. You want to come, don't you?
Polly Try stopping me. I'm due some holiday. I'll just go and tell the landlord and pack my things.

They embrace

Polly exits into the Inn

Robinson runs off R

Villainous music as Blackbeard creeps on from DL, *followed by Patch*

Blackbeard (*laughing his grisly laugh*) Ha har! Hee hee! Old Flint's treasure, ey! 'Tis gonna be mine, I tell ee! All mine! Ha har!
Patch But '*ow*, Cap'n? We ain't got the map an' we ain't got a ship!
Blackbeard No, but *they* 'ave! Listen. All we 'as to do is get a berth on yonder ship. Let 'em find the treasure for us! Then we slit their gizzards—take over the ship an' collar the booty! Ha har!
Patch Just the two of us?
Blackbeard Ar! 'Twill be child's play! (*He turns* US)
Patch (*to the audience*) I wish I'd never left [local firm]!

Two sailors enter on the ship from UR

(*Going to Blackbeard*) But, Cap'n—'ow are we gonna get aboard?
Blackbeard You leave that to me. (*To the sailors, very affable*) Ahoy there, shipmates! A fine lookin' craft!

The sailors come down the gangplank

First Sailor Ay, she is that.
Blackbeard When do ee sail?
Second Sailor Very soon.
Blackbeard Will ee be takin' on any more crew?
First Sailor No. We've got a full ship's company.
Blackbeard (*touching a forelock*) Thank ee kindly, mateys.

The two sailors exit L

Blackbeard draws an ugly-looking dagger from his belt

Act I, Scene 1

After 'em!!

Blackbeard runs out L

Patch (*to the audience*) Oh, no!

Patch gulps and trots out after Blackbeard

Two loud splashes are heard from off L

Blackbeard enters, laughing his grisly laugh, followed by Patch

Blackbeard Ha har! Hee hee! There be two vacancies on board now, I reckon!

Captain Bowsprit enters on the ship from UR

Captain (*calling orders to off* R) Make ready there! Look lively!

Blackbeard nudges Patch, and they move up to near the gangplank

Blackbeard (*touching his forelock, very servile*) Beggin' yer pardon, Captain. 'Tis about two o' yer crew.
Captain (*coming down the gangplank*) Well?
Blackbeard They've jumped ship, Cap'n. Gone to work for [local place]!
Captain Blisterin' barnacles! Two men short and I'm just about to sail!
Blackbeard Beggin' yer pardon, Cap'n. Me an' my shipmate 'ere be lookin' fer a berth. Would ee take us on?
Captain You! Got any credentials?
Blackbeard We both served under Captain James Cook, sir. Better seamen you've yet to meet.
Captain Captain Cook, eh! Very well. You're hired. Come aboard and I'll sign you on. Jump to it!

Captain goes up the gangplank and exits UR

Blackbeard (*saluting after him*) Thank ee kindly, Cap'n! (*To the audience*) Ha har! 'E'll be the first to get 'is gizzard slit! And then—it'll be *your* turn! Ha har!

Blackbeard goes up the gangplank and exits. Patch follows

Noise and bustle is heard off stage, and the Chorus enter from all directions

Willy and Bessie enter from R. Both are comically dressed for the seaside. Willy wears huge Bermuda shorts and Bessie carries a bucket and spade

Comic business as they parade about. The Chorus laugh

Willy If you think we look daft, wait until you see Ma!

Ma Crusoe enters from R. She is ludicrously dressed for sailing and covered with water wings, life belts, etc.

Ma (*dancing about and singing*) "A life on the ocean waves..." (*To the audience, indicating the life belts, etc.*) Well, you can't be too careful, can you, dear! I've seen that *Titanic* ten times!

The Captain enters on the deck of the ship

Captain (*barking at them*) Avast there! Jump to it! Time to be casting off!

The Captain exits UR

Ma Castin' off? Funny time to start knittin'! (*She suddenly panics*) Where's our Robinson? We can't go without him!

Robinson enters from R with a kit bag over his shoulder

Robinson Here I am, Ma!
Ma 'Urry up, lad! The Captain's got 'is engine runnin'!
Robinson (*looking about*) Where's Polly? Ah! Here she is.

Polly comes out of the Inn. She wears a cloak and carries a small bundle. She is not looking very happy

(*Going to her*) Come on, Polly. We're about to sail. What's the matter?
Polly Oh, Robbie. I'm afraid I won't be coming with you after all. I've just had a message. It's Grandmother. She's been taken ill again. I'm really sorry, but I must go to her. You do understand.
Robinson (*crestfallen*) Yes—of course.
Polly (*near to tears*) Goodbye—have a nice trip—think of me.

Polly kisses his cheek, and tearfully runs out L

Ma (*putting a comforting arm around him*) Never mind, Robbie. You'll only be gone a couple of years. (*With hushed tones*) And just think what a whoppin' great present you'll be bringin' 'er back.

Act I, Scene 2

Robinson (*brightening*) That's true.

The Captain enters on the ship

Captain All aboard! All aboard *The Dancing Dolphin*!

Song 4

A lively song and dance for everyone

It ends with Robinson, Ma, Willy and Bessie boarding the ship

The gangplank is pulled up and ropes are released etc. The Chorus turn US *to watch the departure. Everyone is waving and cheering, as the Lights fade to Black-out. Jolly nautical music to cover the scene change*

Scene 2

Below deck

Tabs, or a frontcloth showing timbered bulkhead, portholes and shipboard paraphernalia

Villainous music, as Blackbeard enters from DL, *followed by Patch*

They are met by the usual barrage of abuse from the audience

Blackbeard (*snarling at the audience*) Gerrrah!! Just you wait, you scurvy land lubbers! Once this ship be mine I'll slit yer gizzards! Ha har! Then I'll rip out yer entrails! Ha har! Then I'll throw what's left of ee to the sharks! Ha har!
Patch (*holding his stomach and looking sick*) Oow! Cap'n! Why do you 'ave to be so blood-thirsty?!
Blackbeard Cos I be a big, brutal, black 'earted, bloodcurdlin' buccaneer, thas why! 'Tis my job! An' I love it! (*He snarls and growls at the audience*) Gerrrah!! Gerrrah!!

The audience snarl back. Repeat business

(*To Patch*) See! Thas 'ow 'tis done! You try!
Patch (*to the audience, really pathetic*) Ger! Nasty! Ger!
Blackbeard Bah! You ain't no fun! You'm boring! 'Tis *all* borin'! I be bored out o' me skull an' crossbones!

Patch You won't be bored when we find that treasure, Cap'n.
Blackbeard Ar! The treasure! But when?! We bin at sea a month now! When be us gonna reach the island, that's what I wants to know!
Patch I'll wager Ma Crusoe knows.
Blackbeard Ar! (*He draws a dagger*) I'll get the old trout to tell me!
Patch Not *that* way, Cap'n! Coax it out of her. Be nice.
Blackbeard Nice! 'Ave you seen 'er! She makes Darth Maul look like [current goodlooker]. I'll coax 'er wi' *this*! (*He brandishes the dagger*)
Patch An' 'ave 'er run screamin' to the others! They'll clap us in irons afore you can say Robert Newton! No, do it my way, Cap'n. I'll 'elp ee. 'Ere she comes.

They clear to L *and lurk partly out of sight*

Ma Crusoe enters from DR. *She is wearing another comical nautical outfit*

Ma (*singing*) "All the nice girls love a sailor, all the nice girls love a tar..." (*She spots the audience*) Oh! Ahoy there, me hearties! Decided to come along for the ride, 'ave ya? Well, I 'ope you've brought yer sea legs with ya. (*To someone*) Oh, yes! I can see *you* 'ave, dear. Proper sea legs they are! All green an' wavey! Ha! Ha! (*To all*) I can't say I'm enjoyin' it much! All this up an' down—up an' down! An' the salt water's playin' havoc with me confection! I can't wait to get on dry land again. Good old terracotta! And it won't be long now. The Captain says we should reach the island by... (*She stops herself*) Oh, no, I mustn't say, must I? Absolute secrecy! You never know who's listenin'!

Blackbeard and Patch emerge and creep up behind her

(*To the audience*) Is there someone listenin'?

"Yes" from the audience

Is there? Where?

"Behind you!" from the audience. Comic business with Ma turning around and the Pirates keeping behind her. At last she comes face to face with Blackbeard

Ahhhgh!! It's [topical nasty on TV/film]!

Positions are—Ma on R, *Blackbeard* C *and Patch on* L

Blackbeard (*threateningly*) Why, you old...!

Act I, Scene 2   21

Patch (*aside, restraining him*) Remember, be nice to 'er—be nice.
Blackbeard (*glaring at Patch, then turning to Ma with a sickly grin*) I beg your pardon—young woman.
Ma (*looking around*) Young woman? What young wo... (*To the audience*) Oh! I think 'e means *me!*
Blackbeard Am I obstructing you?
Ma No—(*she flutters her eyelashes at him*) But you can always try!

Blackbeard is at a loss how to continue. Patch prompts him

Patch (*aside*) Tell 'er 'ow beautiful she is.
Blackbeard (*glaring at him, then turning to Ma*) If I said you had a gorgeous body, would you hold it against me?
Ma Oo! You saucy sea dog, you!
Blackbeard I dreamt about you last night.
Ma Did you?
Blackbeard No, you wouldn't let me! Ha har! (*He laughs and gives her a playful push that almost knocks her over*) D'you know, your teeth are like stars.
Ma (*pleased*) They sparkle, you mean?
Blackbeard No, they come out at night! Ha har! (*He laughs and repeats the pushing business*)
Ma (*to the audience*) If 'e does that again, I'll clobber 'im! (*To Blackbeard, ultra posh*) Every morning I stand in front of the mirror and gaze at my beautiful reflection. (*Coyly*) I suppose you'd say I was vain.
Blackbeard No, but I'd say you had a good imagination! Ha har! (*He is about to repeat the push*)

Ma steps back and he falls over. She laughs to the audience. Blackbeard gets up and advances on her in a threatening manner. Patch dives in and pulls him to L

Patch (*aside to him*) You'm goin' about it the wrong way, Cap'n. Leave it to me. (*He saunters over to Ma and coughs politely*) Ahem!
Ma (*reacting at the sight of him; to the audience*) Crikey! Where did [topical personality to suit] spring from?! (*To Patch*) What d'you want?
Patch (*oozing charm*) I really must apologize for my friend. He's a trifle shy.
Ma A trifle shy! 'E looks more like a coconut shy!
Patch It's just his way. He's not very good on water.
Ma No, 'e looks like 'e could do with a bath!
Patch Now, on dry land—say a nice little *desert island* somewhere—he's quite different. A real Romeo! On a nice little *desert island* he'd take you for a date behind the palms. (*He nudges her and winks*)
Ma (*getting interested*) Would 'e? (*To the audience*) Oh, well! Beggars can't

be choosers, eh, girls? (*She crosses to Blackbeard and looks him up and down*) I don't suppose 'e's too bad—once you get past the privet. (*To Patch*) An' 'e's a right goer on dry land, y'say?

Patch nods

> (*To Blackbeard*) Well, you're in luck, lover boy. We'll be stoppin' at an island soon, an'...

Blackbeard (*eagerly moving very close to her*) When?! When?! Tell me!! Tell me!!

Ma (*to the audience*) The affect I 'ave on men! Madonna [or other sex symbol] eat yer 'eart out! (*To Blackbeard*) All right, I'll tell ya. The Captain says... (*She stops. To the audience*) Shall I tell him?

"No!" from the audience

> Shall I?

"No!" from the audience again

Blackbeard (*to the audience*) Oh, yes, she will!

"Oh, no, she won't"/"Oh, yes, she will" routine with the audience. When the routine has run its course, Ma speaks again

Ma No. I can't tell you. Absolute secrecy! My lips are sealed.
Blackbeard Then I'll 'ave to open 'em—wi' this! (*He draws his dagger*)
Ma Oo! That's a big toothpick!
Blackbeard (*advancing on her*) Tell me about the island, you old jellyfish! (*He forces her back against the proscenium arch* R) Tell me, or I'll slit yer gizzard!
Ma (*yelling*) 'Elp! 'Elp!
Patch (*looking off* L) Cap'n! There be someone comin'! Quick!

Patch manages to bundle Blackbeard out DR

Ma clings to the proscenium arch

Willy and Bessie enter from DL

Willy (*going to Ma*) Ma, what's up?
Ma (*clinging to him*) Oow! Willy! I was nearly a goner! One of the crew 'ad a go at me!
Willy Well, you're safe now, cos— (*he strikes a pose*) I'm here!

Act I, Scene 3

Ma (*to the audience*) That's a comfort!
Bessie (*to Ma*) One of the crew, you say. What was he after?
Ma Humph! Not what I thought 'e was after! 'E was only interested in the island!
Willy The island! I 'ope you didn't tell 'im we'll be reachin' it later today!
Ma 'Course not, you stupid boy! 'Ere! You don't think 'e knows about— (sotto voce) The treasure, do ya?
Willy I 'ope not. Captain Bowsprit doesn't want any of the crew knowin'.
Bessie He's afraid they'll turn ugly.
Ma Well, I've got news for 'im! One of 'em already 'as! Oh! I think I'll go for a lie down. Willy, ask that nice young steward to come to my cabin, will ya. (*She moves to the exit* DR)
Willy Yes, Ma. What do you want him to bring you?
Ma Just himself!

With a wink to the audience and a kick of her heel, Ma exits DR

Bessie Oh, Willy! Just think! As soon as we return home with the treasure we can be married! (*She snuggles up to him*) I'm really looking forward to our honeymoon, aren't you? (*She snuggles closer*) Just me—and my little Willy!
Willy (*nervously*) Yes-es!

Song 5

A comedy duet

After the number, they dance off DR, *as the Lights fade to Black-out*

Nautical music to cover the scene change

Scene 3

Deck of The Dancing Dolphin

The ship's bulwarks run right across the back. Note: This should be high enough for the Crimson Hawk and her Pirates to make an effective entrance later. The side wings represent masts, rigging, sails, etc. The backcloth shows a blue sky. A few barrels and boxes are set at the sides and near the bulwarks

Robinson is discovered at the back, looking out to sea through a telescope

Captain Bowsprit enters R

Captain (*going up to him*) Ahoy there, young Crusoe!
Robinson (*lowering the telescope*) Hallo, Captain. (*He points out*) That ship is still there. (*He hands the telescope to Captain*)
Captain (*looking*) Ay! Same one that's been in our wake for days.
Robinson What kind of vessel is she, Captain?
Captain Hard to tell. She ain't flyin' any colours, y'see. (*He lowers the telescope*)
Robinson As long as she's not flying the Jolly Roger, eh.
Captain True! But we've got to keep a weather eye open. These *are* pirate waters, y'know. Don't want to run up against the Crimson Hawk.
Robinson The Crimson Hawk?
Captain Ay! The latest scourge of the Seven Seas! A *woman* too, by all accounts!
Robinson A woman pirate! Surely not.
Captain Why not! Women are well known for their takin' ways! Piracy is a natural career move for 'em!

Both laugh

Robinson (sotto voce) And you still think we'll reach the island later today?
Captain (*patting his pocket;* sotto voce) Accordin' to Flint's map—ay!

Ma Crusoe, Willy and Bessie enter from R

The Chorus, as ship's crew, enter from different directions

Ma (*to the audience, waving*) Ahoy, there, me hearties!

The audience call back

Willy (*to the audience*) Avast behind!
Ma (*to Willy*) Oy! There's no need to get personal! (*She goes to Captain*) Ahoy there, Captain, me old cockle! 'Eaved any yo-ho-ho's lately?

The Captain is stone-faced

(*To the audience*) Crikey! 'E looks like someone's shivered 'is timbers an' spliced 'is main brace! (*To Captain*) Come on, cheer up! We've come to rehearse our big number for the ship's concert tonight. We want you to give it the seal of approval.
Captain Ain't got time! Duties to attend to! (*He makes for the exit* L)
Bessie (*stopping him; pleading*) Oh, please, Daddy! It's very good. Please stay and watch.

Act I, Scene 3   25

Captain Oh ... Very well! (*He sits on a barrel or a box near the* L *wings*) Get on with it!
Ma (*clapping her hands*) Right! Right! Places everyone! Places!

The principals and Chorus scurry into their positions

(*To the conductor/pianist*) Music!!

Song 6

The choice of song and dance routine is left to the individual director. "Disco dancing" might be fun, using taped music and flashing lights. Whatever is chosen, it must give plenty of comic scope for the performers, particularly Ma, Willy and Bessie. A "big finish" is intended, but it ends in comic disaster, with Ma falling back on to the Captain's lap

Ma (*to Captain, with her arms around his neck*) Well? What d'you think?
Captain (*gasping under her weight*) Breathtakin'!

He gets up, causing Ma to fall to the floor. Robinson and Willy help her up

I shall be in my cabin! (*He limps painfully to exit* L) Adjustin' me Captain's log!

Captain limps out L

Laughing, Robinson, Willy, Bessie and the Chorus exit

Ma (*rubbing her hands with glee*) Oo! I can't believe it! Later today we'll be on the island. Diggin' up all that lovely loot! I shall... (*She hears something*) What's that? Thought I 'eard somethin'! (*She tiptoes* L *and looks off*) Oh, no! It's them two nasties! What am I gonna do?! I'd better 'ide! (*She scuttles up and hides behind the* R *wing*)

Villainous music as Blackbeard creeps on from L, *followed by Patch*

Blackbeard Ha har! Did ee 'ear what that old baggage said, Mr Patch! Later today we reach the island! He har! It won't be long now! Soon Flint's treasure will be mine! All mine! Ha har! Ha har!

Ma pokes her head out and listens

(*To the audience, drawing his dagger*) An' as soon as I've collared the booty, I'll slit their gizzards! The Captain! (*He makes a throat-slitting*

gesture) 'Is daughter! (*Another gesture*) An' all that crummy Crusoe family! (*Another gesture*) Ha har!
Ma (*wailing loudly*) Oh, no!! (*She realizes her mistake and quickly withdraws her head*)
Patch (*on the alert*) Hush, Cap'n! I 'eard somefink! There be someone 'ere!

They turn US *and look, then back to the audience*

Blackbeard (*to the audience, brandishing his dagger*) Be there someone 'ere?

"No!" from the audience

Patch
Blackbeard } (*together*) Oh, yes, there is!

After the routine with the audience is repeated a couple of times, Ma sticks her head out and shouts

Ma Oh, no, there isn't!! Ooops!

Too late! The pirates see her and drag her out

(*Struggling*) Y-you won't steal our treasure! I'll tell the others! I'll spill the beans!
Blackbeard *I'll* do the spillin'! (*He puts the dagger to her throat*)
Ma (*casually*) Do you collect stamps?
Blackbeard No!
Ma Well, 'ere's one to start you off! (*She stamps on his toe*)

Yelling in pain, Blackbeard releases her

Ma runs out R

Blackbeard After 'er! Don't let 'er get away!

Blackbeard and Patch run out R

From UR, *behind the bulwarks, the masts and sails of a ship glide into view. It should appear to be a short distance away. When it gets* C, *it stops and the Jolly Roger is hoisted*

Yelling, Ma runs on from R, *hotly pursued by Blackbeard and Patch. They chase her around the deck and out* L

Act I, Scene 3

Over the bulwarks appear a band of Pirates, armed to the teeth with cutlasses and pistols

They drop silently to the deck and crouch, waiting

The dashing, masked figure of the Crimson Hawk slips over the side and descends to the deck

She nonchalantly leans against the bulwarks, toying with her drawn rapier

Yelling, Ma runs on from L, pursued by Blackbeard and Patch

They succeed in grabbing hold of her, Blackbeard R, Patch L. None of them notice the Crimson Hawk or her Pirates

Patch 'Ow be us gonna stop 'er from blabbin', Cap'n?
Blackbeard Easy! We'll throw 'er over the side an' let the sharks take care of it! Ha har!

They drag Ma to DL and prepare to throw her over the side—this being the edge of the stage

Ma (*struggling*) 'Elp! I'm allergic to water! 'Elp!!

Quickly, the Crimson Hawk moves down and lays the point of her sword on Blackbeard's right shoulder. The Pirates move down

Hawk (*loud and clear*) I wouldn't do that if I were you, my furry friend!

Blackbeard and Patch stop struggling with Ma. Blackbeard turns his head and is confronted with the sword point. Patch sees the Pirates surrounding them

Be so good as to let the lady go—(*with a little jab of the sword point*) If you please.

Blackbeard and Patch release Ma, and she scuttles to R of the Crimson Hawk

Boys!

Two of the Pirates grab Blackbeard and Patch and drag them L, where they cover them with pistols. One disarms Blackbeard. Crimson Hawk sheaths her sword and turns to Ma

You are quite safe now, ma'am.

Captain Bowsprit, Robinson, Willy, Bessie and a couple of the crew enter from R

Ma rushes to join them. The other Pirates quickly surround the group with pistols and cutlasses at the ready

Captain What the blazes! (*To Hawk*) Who the devil are you?! What are you doin' aboard my ship?!
Hawk Allow me to introduce myself. I am—(*she strikes a pose*) the Crimson Hawk!

Dramatic chords of music

Robinson The female pirate!

Ma and the others react

Blackbeard (*snarling*) So! You be the Crimson Hawk, eh?!
Hawk I am! And you, if I'm not mistaken, are the infamous Blackbeard!
Ma & Others Blackbeard!!
Blackbeard (*boastfully*) Ar! The scourge of the Seven Seas!
Hawk Not any more!

Hawk and her Pirates roar with laughter. Blackbeard scowls

Captain (*to Hawk*) You've been followin' us for days! Why?
Hawk Out of curiosity, my dear Captain. What could possibly bring a lone ship into these treacherous waters, I asked myself. There must be a very good reason for it. Could it be something to do with—buried treasure?

The others react

Ah! I thought as much! So! It's buried treasure you're after, is it?
Blackbeard (*snarling*) Ar! An' it's *mine*!!
Ma (*snarling back*) No, it's not! It's *ours*!!
Blackbeard Mine!!
Others Ours!!
Blackbeard Mine!!
Others Ours!!
Hawk (*holding up her arm; shouting*) Belay!!

They go silent

Act I, Scene 3

Allow me to settle the argument for you. It's now—*mine!*

Loud protests from all of the interested parties. Hawk calls for order again

Silence!

They go silent

Now! Whenever there's buried treasure, there's always a map. Kindly hand it over.

The others look away, pretending not to be there

Very well! In that case, I'll ask my boys to search you all—even the ladies!

Horrified reaction from Bessie as a particularly gruesome-looking pirate moves towards her

Pirate (*leering at her*) Ar! Nothin' I like better than a good body search!
Ma (*tapping him on the shoulder*) Me first!
Pirate (*looking at her in disgust*) Even I've got standards! (*He turns back to Bessie, flexing his fingers*)

Bessie gives a terrified squeal

Robinson I think you'd better hand over the map, Captain.

The Captain takes the map from his pocket and hands it to the Hawk. She motions the pirate away

Pirate Humph! Spoilsport! (*He slouches back to his cronies*)

Hawk holds up the map, triumphantly. Her Pirates give a cheer

Captain (*to Hawk*) And now I suppose you'll slaughter us!
Hawk Certainly not. You are all free to go on your way, unharmed and with my blessing. I'll relieve you of your treasure, but not your lives. Unnecessary violence and killing is not part of my piratical code! (*To Blackbeard*) Unlike some! (*To Captain*) I strongly advise you to clap that overgrown cactus in irons! And now... (*She strides to the bulwarks and turns*) The Crimson Hawk bids ye farewell! A thousand thanks for your company and—*this!* (*She waves the map. To Pirates*) Come, my brave buckos! There's treasure to be found!

Lithely, the Crimson Hawk slips over the bulwarks and vanishes. Cheering, her pirate band follow her over the side

The others rush to the bulwarks and look over. Blackbeard and Patch lurk DL. During the following, the pirate ship glides out of sight, UL

Patch *(in a panic)* What be us gonna do, Cap'n?! They'll swing us from the yard-arm!
Blackbeard No, they won't! They'll be too busy drownin'! Quick! Go an' lower the rowin' boat an' wait fer me! I'll be in the powder magazine— lightin' a fuse! *(To the audience)* I be gonna blow up this 'ere ship an' send 'em all to Davy Jones Locker! Ha har!

Blackbeard runs out L, followed by Patch

Ma, Robinson, the Captain and the crew turn away from the bulwarks. Willy and Bessie continue looking out to sea

Ma Cor! What a woman! An' that outfit of 'ers! 'Ere! D'you think I'd look good in one of those? *(She mimics the Hawk's walk and stance. Then, grumpily)* Not that I'll be able to buy a flippin' thing now we've said goodbye to the treasure!
Robinson We had to give her the map, Ma. Who knows what those pirates might have subjected you and Bessie to.
Ma Well, I'll never find out now, will I! Oh, I suppose you're right, Robbie ... At least old Blackpuddin' didn't get 'is mucky maulers on it! *(She looks L)* Oy! Where is 'e? Where's 'e gone?!
Captain *(to a crew member)* Search the ship! I want Blackbeard in irons!
Willy *(calling and pointing over the side)* Look!! Look!! It's Blackbeard!!

The others rush to the bulwarks and look over

Captain By thunder! He's taken the rowin' boat!
Robinson He's getting away!
Ma *(shouting)* Good riddance to bad rubbish! *(She shakes her fist)*
Blackbeard *(off, from behind the bulwarks)* I 'ope you enjoy the fireworks!
Captain *(yelling back)* Fireworks?! What the devil d'you mean?!
Blackbeard *(off)* Ha har! You'll soon find out!

From off L there is a blinding flash. It is followed by a deafening explosion. Ma, Willy and Bessie scream and cling to each other. The Captain and Robinson rush to L and look off. From off L comes a cloud of smoke and the flickering of flames is seen

Act I, Scene 4

The rest of the crew rush on

Robinson Captain! What is it?!
Captain Blisterin' barnacles! He's blown up the ship's powder magazine! We're done for! (*He yells the order*) Abandon ship!! Abandon ship!!

From off L, there comes another flash and explosion. The whole stage is now filled with red, flickering fire effects. Smoke swirls. Absolute chaos breaks out. Everyone is yelling and being thrown about. At the same time—whistles blow, wind howls, waves crash, thunder rolls and lightening flashes. The works! Loud, tempestuous music joins in for good measure. Ma, Willy and Bessie all try to get into the same life belt. When the pandemonium is at its height, there is a complete Black-out

The tempestuous music continues during the scene change, then it changes to a tranquil theme as the Lights come up on

Scene 4

Adrift at sea

Tabs, or a frontcloth showing the sky and a flat, calm sea

Right across the front runs a ground row of stylized waves. Behind this, C, is an old-fashioned bath tub (cutout). It has a makeshift mast with a pair of frilly bloomers (wired out) for a sail

Sitting in the "bath" are Ma Crusoe C, Willy L and Bessie R. They are unsuccessfully trying to paddle the "bath" with a tennis racket, a fly swatter and a toilet brush

Ma (*giving up*) Oh, this is bloomin' 'opeless! We've bin goin' round in circles for hours! We're getting nowhere with these stupid things!

They throw their "paddles" overboard, US. They make a clatter as they land

(*To the audience*) Must be hard water!

A moment of gloomy silence

Willy I wish I 'ad a couple of big oars!
Ma (*shocked*) Willy Crusoe!

Willy (*doing "rowing" action*) Then I could row properly.
Ma Ah!

Bessie starts crying

Oh, no! Don't start cryin' again, Bessie! We've only just bailed out from your last downpour!
Bessie (*between sobs*) I can't help it... I keep thinking of poor Daddy—and Robinson—and the others—all drowned! Waaah!

Willy starts crying as well, then Ma joins in. All three wail loudly, then Willy sees something out front

Willy (*pointing*) Look!! What's that?
Ma (*looking*) It... It looks like land!
Bessie It must be the island!

They cheer, excitedly

Ma Come on, you two! All we've got to do is row to the island an' we're saved!
Bessie And how are we going to do that? We threw away our paddles, remember!
Willy The island's not that far away. We can swim for it!
Ma Swim for it! Who d'you think I am—[well-known swimmer]? Besides, I 'aven't brought me cossie!
Willy Don't worry about that, Ma. You can swim in your underwear!
Ma Oh, no, I can't! (*She points to the bloomers on the mast*) And if you think I'm swimmin' in me birthday suit, forget it! The water's like ice! I'm not endin' up with frozen assets! Any 'ow, you're forgettin' somethin', action man! What about—*sharks*!!
Bessie (*looking about, frightened*) Oo, yes! S-she's right, Willy!
Willy There aren't any sharks here! (*To the audience*) Are there, folks?

From off DR, *a large shark fin appears above the waves, in a follow spot. The theme music from* Jaws *is played. The audience will be shouting "Look! It's a shark!", etc. Willy and the others don't see it*

(*To the audience*) Oh, no, there isn't!

"Oh, yes, there is!" from the audience, and the routine follows. During this, the shark fin glides across and stops in front of the bath. Eventually the three of them see it, and yell in fright

Act I, Scene 4   33

   Aaagh!! It's a sh-sh-shark!!
Ma Shoo! Go away! The bathroom's occupied! Go away! Ooo! What are we gonna do?!
Bessie Daddy told me once that singing sometimes frightens sharks away!
Ma Singin'! Well, anythin's worth a try! What shall we sing to it?
Willy Anything—except "food, glorious food"!
Bessie Let's try—[a well-known nursery rhyme or something everyone will know]!

They sing in timid, quavering voices. The shark doesn't move

Ma Oo! It's still there! It's not goin' away!
Bessie I don't think we sang loud enough. Let's try again!

They sing again, a little louder. The shark still doesn't move

Willy We're still not loud enough. (*To the audience*) Folks, will you help us?

"Yes" from the audience

   Good! Sing as loud as you can to frighten off the shark! One—two—three!

They sing with the audience and encourage them to sing louder, etc. Finally, the shark fin glides off DL *and disappears. Willy and the others cheer*

   It worked! (*He gives the audience a thumbs-up sign*) Thanks, folks!
Ma What if it comes back!
Willy (*to the audience*) You'll warn us, won't you, kids?

"Yes" from the audience

The shark fin appears from DL. *The audience shout to warn the others. The fin glides* C. *The three start singing and encourage the audience to join in. The shark fin glides off* DR. *All cheer. The fin re-appears and glides to* C. *Repeat singing and shark going away business ad lib. Finally, the shark remains* C *and does not go away*

Ma It's not goin' away any more!
Bessie What are we going to do now?!
Willy I'll try throwin' somethin' at it! (*He quickly picks up "something"—in fact nothing—from the bottom of the bath. He throws "it" at the shark fin*)

Loud cymbal crash from the band! The fin makes a very quick exit

Bulls eye!

They cheer and watch the fin's departure

Ma Cor! Look at it go! Well done, Willy! What did you throw at it?
Willy Oh, just something in the bottom of the bath.
Ma (*looking down*) Just something... (*Horror-struck*) Oh, no!! You stupid twit! That *something* was the bath plug! You pulled the plug out!!
All (*yelling, to out front*) Help!!

Quick Black-out. Sound effect of water gurgling down a plug hole is heard. Music to cover the scene change

SCENE 5

King Neptune's Palace Under the Sea

This scene should be full of enchantment and fantasy. The set designer and lighting team can have a field day! The side wings and ground row represent columns of colourful coral and fantastic underwater plants. A shimmering, blueish-green backcloth. UCL *is a shell-shaped throne*

King Neptune is seated on his throne. He is suffering from a bad cold and keeps dabbing his nose with a large handkerchief. His trident leans against the throne. The Chorus, as aquatic attendants, are posed around. The dancers and children, as sea horses, anemones, small fish and other underwater life, are performing a dance. The Chorus can accompany the dance with singing if desired

Song 7

After the number, they all turn to Neptune and bow. He gives an enormous sneeze, causing some of the smaller ones to fall over. Sneezing again, Neptune waves them aside

A dignified Attendant enters from R, *goes to the throne and bows*

Attendant Your Majesty...
Neptune (*sneezing*) Achoooo!!

The Attendant gets sprayed

(*Wiping his nose*) Oh, curse these confounded colds! It's one after the

Act I, Scene 5   35

other! Will I never be free of them?! It's the damp y'see! Still, what can you expect living on the seabed all your life! (*To Attendant*) Well? What do you want?
Attendant Your Majesty...
Neptune (*sneezing*) Achoooo!!

The Attendant gets sprayed again

(*To Attendant*) Well? Speak up! Speak up!
Attendant Your Majesty, I have to report that a human being has entered your kingdom.
Neptune A *live* one?
Attendant Yes, sire. A party of mermaids rescued him from drowning and brought him here.
Neptune I see. Oh, well, I suppose I'd better see this human! (*He brightens up*) Who knows! He might be able to cure my cold! Bring him before me! (*He sneezes*) Achoooo!!

The Attendant gets sprayed yet again

The Attendant exits R

Neptune sneezes again

The Attendant returns, followed by Robinson

Robinson gazes about him in wonderment and delight

Robinson Wow! Neptune's palace under the sea!
Attendant (*to Robinson, sternly*) Bow to His Majesty.
Robinson (*to the audience*) And they speak English! What a stroke of luck! (*He goes up to the throne and bows to Neptune*) Your Majesty.
Neptune (*sneezing*) Achoooo!!
Robinson Bless you.
Neptune Eh? What did you say?
Robinson I said "bless you", Your Majesty. Where I come from we always say "bless you" if someone sneezes.
Neptune (*intrigued*) Do you really? And does it cure a cold?
Robinson I'm not sure, but at least it shows someone cares.
Neptune (*mulling it over*) Mm... Bless you... Yes... Yes, I like it! (*He indicates his court*) No-one here seems to care very much! (*To all*) From now on, whenever I sneeze, you will all say "bless you"!
Others (*bowing*) Yes, Your Majesty.
Neptune (*to Robinson*) Do you have a name?

Robinson Yes, sire. It's Robinson Crusoe. I'm very grateful to your beautiful mermaids for saving me from drowning.
Neptune (*dismissively*) Oh, that's all right. They've made a habit of it. They're always... (*He sneezes*) Achoooo!!
Others Bless you!
Neptune Well done! Now, Robinson Crusoe, how came you to be drowning in my ocean?
Robinson I was travelling on a ship with my family and friends. We were bound for a certain desert island.
Neptune A desert island, eh? (*Matter-of-factly*) After buried treasure, no doubt.

Robinson reacts

Oh, you needn't look so surprised. It's happening all the time in this part of my domain. What you humans choose to do on dry land does not concern me. Go on with your story.
Robinson Earlier today our ship was boarded by a female pirate called the Crimson Hawk.
Neptune Ah, yes! Reports tell me she is very courteous and extremely humane for a pirate.
Robinson Oh, she is. Granted, she stole our treasure map, but she let us go free and unharmed.
Neptune Then it was not she who caused you the wetting?
Robinson No, sire. That was another pirate! He pretended to be one of the crew and was plotting to steal the treasure for himself. When we discovered his plan—he blew up the ship! His name is Blackbeard!
Neptune (*rising in anger*) Blackbeard! That villain! Of all the pirates who pollute my Seven Seas he is by far the worst! For many years he has strewn my sea beds with burnt-out wrecks of ships! He's not only a vicious vandal, he's a litter bug! (*He calms down and sits*) You spoke of family and friends. What has become of them?
Robinson I don't know. I lost sight of them when we jumped overboard. (*Sadly*) I ... I expect they were all drowned.
Neptune (*to Attendant*) Have there been reports of any... Er...? (*He points downwards*)
Attendant Not today, sire.
Neptune (*to Robinson*) Then it appears they reached dry land in safety. Very probably this desert island you spoke of.
Robinson I hope so!
Neptune And presumably you wish to join them?
Robinson Very much, Your Majesty.
Neptune Then I will... (*He is struck by a thought*) Wait a minute! (*A revelation*) Jumping jelly fish!! Do you realise I haven't sneezed for

Act I, Scene 5

several minutes! And... (*He sniffs*) Yes! I do believe my cold has completely vanished! Ha! Ha! (*Overjoyed, he tosses away his handkerchief; and rises*) Robinson Crusoe, this "bless you" of yours has worked! I'm indebted to you! (*He takes up his trident and gives a command*) Summon my fastest sea serpent at once!

The Attendant runs out R

Neptune comes down to Robinson

It will carry you to the surface and place you safely on the island's shore!
Robinson (*bowing*) Thank you, Your Majesty.
Neptune Good Robinson Crusoe, you have cured my cold.
I wish you luck in your search for gold.
Robinson It would be nice to find the treasure,
But to find my family would give greater pleasure.
(*Out front*)) Will this adventure end in folly?
Should I have stayed at home with Polly?
It's too late now to change my mind.
Let's hope the Fates will all be kind.
To face the future I must be strong!
Neptune So let's have a song to help him along!

Song 8

This should be a stirring song for Robinson and the Chorus

During it, a very friendly-looking sea serpent makes its entrance. (See Production Notes)

The music continues under Robinson's final speech

Robinson Away I go to a desert isle!
Will it be good or will it be vile?
To see what thrills I must undertake,
You'll have to wait until after the break!

Music up and the singing is resumed. Robinson is helped on to the serpent's back. It ends with a grand tableau, as——

—*the* CURTAIN *falls*

ACT II

Scene 1

The Desert Island

Side wings and ground row representing palm trees, exotic plants and jungle creepers, etc. The backcloth shows the jungle framing a distant view of the sea. A large rock is UR

To the dreamy strains of By the Sleepy Lagoon *(Desert Islands Discs theme music) The* CURTAIN *rises*

The stage is empty. Bird song and the chatter of monkeys is heard. All looks peaceful and serene in the dappled sunlight

Suddenly, a large Gorilla lands on the stage from off L *or it can make its entrance from the back of the auditorium, causing havoc with the audience on its way to the stage. It takes a large banana from the wings and proceeds to "unzip" it*

The rhythmic beat of distant drums is heard

The Gorilla cocks its head and listens

The Gorilla "re-zips" the banana, and with a grunt to the audience, bounds out DL

The drum beats grow louder

From R *and* L, *the Chorus and dancers, as Islanders, shuffle-dance on to the beat of the drum. They go into a song and dance routine*

Song 9

This can start as a simple tribal dance, then develop into something completely out of character with the setting—i.e.—a Broadway-style all singin', all dancin' type extravaganza

Act II, Scene 1

After the number, the drum beats continue

A fearsome Medicine Man leaps on from R to C

The Islanders form a semi-circle around him

He points to R with his skull wand

Medicine Man (*yelling*) *Abooga Boya!! Abooga Boya!!*

From R, a young Islander, later to be known as Man Friday, is dragged on by two other Islanders. He is very frightened

The other Islanders start a low chant and take up threatening stances. The Medicine Man moves to L and points C. The two Islanders drag Friday to C, throw him to the ground then join the others. Friday crouches in terror as the Medicine Man circles around him, shaking his wand. The Medicine Man leaps to L and raises his arms. The drum beats and chanting stop abruptly. A deathly silence

(*Pointing to Friday*) *Kala!! Boogar!!*

Silently, the Islanders close in on the cringeing Friday

Robinson (*off L, calling*) Hallo! Is there anybody there?! Ma! Billy! Hallo!

On hearing this, the Islanders react. At a signal from the Medicine Man, they all run out R

Friday leaps to his feet and runs out DL

Robinson enters from UL

(*Calling*) Hallo! (*Desperately*) Oh, if there's anyone here, please answer me! Hallo! (*He shrugs and moves DC. He sees the audience*) Hi, folks! Well, this island seems to be completely deserted. I haven't seen a soul since Neptune's sea serpent dumped me on the shore. Perhaps Ma and the others are on a different island. I don't even know if this is the one where the treasure's buried. Tch! What a mess! I wish I'd never... (*He looks down*) Hey! Look at this! Footprints! Loads of 'em! That proves there must be someone here! I'll follow them and see what happens. I hope they'll lead me to someone friendly. Wish me luck!

Following the prints, Robinson exits UR

Friday creeps on from DL *and follows Robinson out*

The Gorilla enters DL *and follows Friday out*

Villainous music as Blackbeard and Patch enter from DR, *dragging Captain Bowsprit between them. He is bound with ropes. Blackbeard now sports a huge cutlass*

They move C

Blackbeard Ha har! (*He sees the audience and snarls at them*) Gerrrah!! Look, Mr Patch! Them scurvy landlubbers be still 'ere!
Patch (*to the audience, very affably*) Oh, hallo! Awfully nice to see you again... (*He waves*) Hallo... hallo...
Blackbeard (*roaring at him*) Belay!! Stow that bilge! They bain't on our side!
Patch Oh, no, I forgot! (*To the audience, with pathetic aggression*) Ger! Nasty! Nasty! Ger!
Blackbeard (*sneering*) So, Captain! 'Ere we be on the Treasure Island! 'Twere a stroke o' luck us picking you up in the rowin' boat. Now you can lead us to the treasure afore that interferin' female gets 'er 'ands on it!
Patch 'Ow can 'e, Cap'n? The Crimson 'Awk took the map!
Blackbeard I knows that, ya crazy cuttlefish! But our fine Captain 'ere 'as got a good memory, I'll lay to that. I reckon 'e could take us to the booty wi' 'is eyes shut! (*He puts the cutlass to Captain's throat*) An' take us 'e will!
Captain Never! D'you hear—never! You sank my ship! Drowned my daughter! I've nothin' left worth livin' for—but I'll *never* tell you where the treasure is! Never!
Blackbeard Then I'll 'ave to put ee to the torture!
Patch (*grimacing*) Oh, no!
Blackbeard (*to Captain*) You'll soon tell when you 'ear what diabolical tortures I learnt at the Piracy evenin' classes in [local place]!
Captain Do your worst, you pirate scum! (*Standing to attention*) I'll never tell!
Patch (*admiringly*) 'E's ever so brave, Cap'n. 'E's got guts!
Blackbeard Ar! But 'e won't 'ave for much longer! Ha har! Come on!

They drag the Captain out DL

Robinson, still following the footprints, enters UR *and exits* UL. *Friday follows him on and out* UL. *The Gorilla follows Friday and exits* UL

Ma Crusoe creeps on backwards from DR. *Her costume is now in tatters, and has seaweed and starfish, etc. hanging from it*

Act II, Scene 1

Ma (*seeing the audience*) Oh, hallo, folks! I see you've found the island as well. We managed to swim ashore, even with that nasty old shark nibblin' at our number plates! (*Business with the back of the costume*) I'm sure 'e took a bite outa my bumper! Oh! Swimmin' those last two miles was agony! We 'adn't realized we'd reached dry land! (*Business*) Oo! I've got sand where you wouldn't believe! (*She looks about in disgust*) An' this island! Well, I wouldn't want to spend me 'olidays 'ere! There's no-one about! Not even [TV holiday programme presenter]! An' now Willy and Bessie 'ave wandered off leavin' me on me own! That's not very nice of them, is it?

She engages in byplay with the audience, then hears something

Shh! Shh! I thought I 'eard a rustlin'! (*She calls, timidly*) Hallo!
Willy (*off L, in a deep voice*) Hallo!
Ma Oh! (*She calls a little louder*) Hallo again!
Willy (*off*) Hallo again!
Ma (*to the audience*) D'you think there's someone there, or is it just an echo?

"There's someone there" from the audience

I don't think there is! I'll put it to the test. (*She calls*) Hallo!
Willy (*off*) Hallo!
Ma I know where——
Willy (*off*) I know where——
Ma I can get——
Willy (*off*) I can get——
Ma Mars bars for five pence!

Willy and Bessie rush on from L. Both their costumes are in comical tatters

Willy Where?! Where?!
Ma (*rounding on him*) Oh! Willy Crusoe! It was you all the time! Don't go wanderin' off again! (*Suspiciously*) 'Ere! What were you two doin' in them bushes anyway?
Bessie (*acting all soppy with Willy*) Willy and I were doing some exploring. Weren't we, Willy?

Willy nods and gives a stupid grin

Ma Well, don't! 'E's not used to foreign parts! 'E breaks out in a cold sweat if 'e walks past a travel agent's window!
Willy We were just tryin' to find out if there was anyone else on the island.
Ma Well, don't bother! This place is like the space between *your* ear 'oles—

empty! Let's face it—(*dramatically*) we're macarooned on an uninhibited island!

All three start crying. Comic business as Ma gives Willy some seaweed to cry into

(*Pulling herself together and trying to rally the others*) Come on! Let's be brave! We mustn't give way! We're *British*, remember! Willy Crusoe! Let me see your stiff upper thing!
Willy (*reacting*) Eh?!!
Ma Your stiff upper lip! Show me!

Comic business as Willy contorts his face to achieve a stiff upper lip

Bessie I know one thing that'll keep our spirits up.
Ma I prefer to keep my spirits down! What's that, then? (*To the audience*) I feel a song comin' on!
Bessie We can sing!
Ma (*to the audience*) What did I tell ya!

Song 10

A comedy song and dance routine for Ma, Willy and Bessie

If desired, the Island Dancers could creep on unseen at the back and copy the dance steps. If so, they exit after the number

Bessie (*to Ma*) Has that raised your spirits?
Ma (*gasping*) No—just me blood pressure!
Willy Y'know, I can't believe that this whole island is deserted. There must be someone 'ere! What about the locals?
Bessie (*getting scared*) Y-you mean—Islanders?!
Willy (*clinging to her*) Y-y-yes!

Unseen by them, the Medicine Man and Islanders creep on at the back

Ma Oh, you pair of wallies! There aren't any Islanders 'ere! (*To the audience*) Are there, kids?

"Yes!" from the audience

Oh, no, there aren't!

Routine with the audience

Act II, Scene 1   43

The Medicine Man and Islanders creep up behind them

Well, I 'aven't seen any! Where are they?

"Behind you!" from the audience

Oh, no, there aren't!

During the responses, the Medicine Man stands right next to her. Willy and Bessie see him and the Islanders. They back away to L and cower in mute terror. Oblivious, Ma continues her argument with the audience

Well, I don't believe you! I 'aven't seen any Islanders! (*To Medicine Man*) 'Ave you seen any—*aaaahg*!!
Medicine Man (*yelling at her*) Abooga!! Abooga!!

Ma runs across to Willy and Bessie

Ma 'E called me abooga!

They cling to each other in terror. The Medicine Man signals to the Islanders. They close in on the terrified trio with knives raised to strike

Suddenly, the Crimson Hawk appears on the rock, UR

She fires a pistol in the air

The Medicine Man and Islanders scream in fright and run out in all directions

Look! It's the Purple Parrot! Or whatever 'er name is!
Hawk (*jumping down from the rock*) Greetings! (*She puts the pistol in her belt*) So! Once again the Crimson Hawk comes to your rescue.
Ma Oh, you can say that again! Ta ever so. Another minute an' we'd 'ave been pincushions!
Hawk But why are you here on this island? I set you free to return home.
Willy (*going to Hawk*) It was that rotten Blackbeard's doin'! As soon as you left 'e blew up our ship!
Bessie We all had to jump overboard. The three of us managed to swim ashore. We don't know what happened to my father or Robinson.
Hawk Robinson? Do you mean the young man who was so sensible about giving me the map?
Ma That's 'im. My son! Oh, I'd give away a *thousand* treasure maps just to know 'e was safe an' sound.

Hawk Quite ... quite. (*She takes the map from her sash*) Well, with the aid of his map I am now searching this island for the treasure.

Slight pause

May I make a suggestion?
Willy Be as suggestive as you like.
Hawk As the Islanders here don't seem to be very friendly, why don't you come along with me and place yourselves under my protection.

The others look at each other, uncertain

Be honest, my friends, do you have a choice—if you want to stay alive that is. Join me, and who knows, we may find the rest of your party along the way.
Ma Y'mean—you'll look after us?
Hawk Ay! My body is yours! (*She strikes a pose with legs apart, hands on hips and chest thrust out. The latter almost touching Willy's nose*)
Willy (*to the audience*) Cor!! (*He turns back to ogle the Hawk*)

Bessie reacts

Hawk (*putting a reassuring hand on his shoulder*) You'll be quite safe as long as you stick to me.
Willy (*drooling*) *Stick* to you! Oh, you bet! Just squeeze my tube and call me Mr Uhu!
Bessie (*pulling him away*) Oy! You're already stuck—with *me*!
Hawk Then I take it you accept my offer. You are prepared to place yourselves in my hands?
Willy (*eagerly*) Oh, yeah!!
Bessie (*snapping at him*) Willy!
Ma (*to Hawk*) Well, I don't fancy waitin' around 'ere to get pricked like a sausage! Yes! We'll go with you. My body is yours! (*She tries to copy the Hawk's pose with comic results. To the audience*) Well! It worked for 'er!
Hawk (*consulting the map*) Now, let me see—ah, yes! This way! (*She moves* DR) And remember—stick close to me at all times.
Willy (*rushing over and standing very close to her*) Ay ay, Captain!
Bessie (*getting between them*) Not *that* close!
Hawk Forward! Follow me!

Hawk strides out DR, *followed by Bessie and Willy*

Ma brings up the rear

Act II, Scene 2

Ma (*to the audience, pausing at the exit*) Girl power, eh! Wish I 'ad some of it! Ta-ta! See you later—I ope!

Ma exits DR

Robinson, still following the footprints, enters UL. He gets to C, shrugs despondently and comes down to address the audience

Robinson I give up, folks. These footprints don't lead anywhere! I've just been going round in circles. Y'know, it's very strange. I haven't seen a single soul, but I've got the distinct feeling I'm being watched. It's creepy. I've been told that tropical nights can get very cold. I'd better build myself some kind of shelter, I suppose. And find some food! But from where? No chance of a Tesco around here! (*He shrugs*) Oh, well! I'll see what I can find. See you later, folks.

Robinson waves and exits R

Friday creeps on from L, and follows Robinson out

The Gorilla enters and follows Friday out—as the Lights fade to Black-out

Music to cover the scene change

Scene 2

Another Part of the Island

Tabs, or a front cloth showing jungle undergrowth, palm trees, creepers, etc.

Villainous music as Blackbeard and Patch enter from DL, dragging Captain Bowsprit between them

Blackbeard Ha har! (*He snarls at the audience*) Gerrrah!!

The audience snarl back

Patch (*to the audience, doing his feeble best*) Ger!
Captain (*to Blackbeard, mockingly*) Well, you pirate scum! Your first torture didn't make me crack, did it?
Blackbeard (*scowling*) Bah! It would 'ave done if that idiot 'ad done the job properly! (*To Patch*) You were supposed to put 'is feet in *boilin'* oil not *baby* oil!

Patch Sorry, Cap'n. (*He conceals a "Mutley" type chuckle*)
Blackbeard I'll take care of the next torture meself! (*To Patch*) 'Ave you got the worms?
Patch No, I always stand like this.
Blackbeard The bag of worms, you barnacled buffoon!
Patch Oh, ar! (*With a look of revulsion, he takes a bag from his pocket*) Ugh!
Blackbeard Ha har! Let's 'ave a look at the little darlin's!
Patch (*grimacing*) Do we 'ave to, Cap'n?
Blackbeard (*roaring*) Arr!

Utterly repulsed, Patch gingerly opens the bag. He swallows hard, screws up his face and reaches into the bag. He brings out several wriggling worms (of the sweet/eatable variety). He holds them at arm's length

(*With devilish glee*) Ha har! Hee! Hee! Just right! All nice an' wriggly an' slimy! (*To Captain*) If you don't tell me where the treasure is, I be gonna put them beauties down yer underpants!
Captain Do what you like! I'll never tell!
Blackbeard So be it! (*He pulls out the front of the Captain's waistband*) Mr Patch—prepare to insert!

Patch moves to the Captain and dangles the "worms" over the extended waistband. The Captain shuts his eyes and grits his teeth. Patch is just about to drop them in, when his arm gives an involuntary jerk, causing the "worms" to fly out into the audience

(*Roaring*) You clumsy swab!!
Patch I couldn't 'elp it, Cap'n! One of 'em was crawlin' up me sleeve! Ugh!
Blackbeard (*to Captain*) Don't think you've got away with it, me bucko! There be still plenty more in the bag! Come on!

Blackbeard drags the Captain out DL

Patch (*to the audience*) Don't eat 'em all at once!

Patch scuttles out DL

The Crimson Hawk enters DR, *studying the map. Ma Crusoe follows, being helped along by Willy*

Ma (*out of breath*) Phew! Any idea 'ow much further it is, Mrs Hawk? Only I'm proper pooped!
Hawk According to the map, the Temple of Boogar should be somewhere in this area.

Act II, Scene 2   47

Willy The temple of *who*-gar?
Hawk Boogar. It's the name of the god the Islanders worship. (*She shows them the map*) Look. There's a drawing of the temple with an idol.
Ma (*looking*) Oh, yes. That must be the idol Boogar.
Willy And the treasure is buried in the temple?
Hawk So the map states— (*she reads*) "Bulk of treasure buried here".
Willy Cor! Isn't it exciting, Bessie... (*He turns to find her not there*) Bessie?! Where is she? She was right behind me a minute ago! (*He panics*) Bessie! Bessie!
Hawk Calm down. There's no need to panic. I expect she stopped to ... er ... you know... (*She winks*)
Willy Get somethin' out of her eye?
Ma Oh, you are a wally, Willy! Let me! (*She whispers in Willy's ear*)

The penny drops

Though with all that cryin' I'm surprised she needs to!
Hawk Look, you two wait here. I'll go back and find her. Don't move from that spot!

Hawk exits DR

Ma and Willy stand rigid, rooted to the spot. A pause

Ma I think we can move about a little bit.

They relax and move DS *together*

Willy I 'ope Bessie's all right, Ma. Those Islanders looked pretty scary.
Ma Yes! Especially their leader! I don't want to meet 'im again!
Willy Me neither!

The Medicine Man and two Islanders creep on from DL

They move to behind Ma and Willy. The audience will be shouting warnings

Ma (*to the audience*) Eh? What's up?
Willy (*to the audience*) I... Is there someone there?

"Yes!" from the audience

Ma
Willy } (*together*) Where?!!

"Behind you!" Comic business with Ma and Willy turning around with the Islanders keeping behind them

Eventually they see the Medicine Man, scream and run out DL, *pursued by the Medicine Man and Islanders*

Bessie enters from DR, *looking scared and lost*

Bessie Ooo! I wish I hadn't stopped to admire those flowers! Now I've lost the others and I don't know what to do! (*She starts crying*)

Blackbeard and Patch enter DL, *dragging Captain Bowsprit*

Captain Bessie!
Bessie Daddy!
Blackbeard Grab 'er, Mr Patch!

Patch grabs Bessie and drags her over

Captain (*to Blackbeard*) You despicable pirate scum! Harm one hair of my daughter's head and I'll...
Blackbeard (*putting the cutlass to his throat*) You'll *what*?! (*He is struck by a devilish thought*) By thunder! That gives me an idea! I'll torture 'er instead! Ar! That'll soon make ee tell us where the treasure is! Bring 'er along! Ha har!

Blackbeard drags the Captain out DL

Bessie wails

Patch drags her out DL

Yelling is heard, and Ma and Willy run on from DR, *pursued by the Medicine Man and two Islanders. They run across and out* DL

Slight pause

The Crimson Hawk enters from DR

Hawk Well, I can't see any sign of Bessie... Oh, shiver me timbers! Ma and Willy have disappeared now! I told them to wait here! (*She calls*) Ma! Willy! (*To the audience*) Did you see what happened to them, shipmates?

The audience shout explanations

Act II, Scene 3

You mean the Islanders are chasing them?

"Yes!" from the audience

Which way did they go?

They tell her and she draws her sword

Thanks, mateys!

The Hawk runs out DL

Slight pause

Yelling is heard, and Ma, Willy, the Medicine Man and Islanders run on from DR

They stop in a line across the stage. They all bend over to get their breath back, then resume the chase off DL

The Gorilla, wearing colourful running shorts and a number, sprints on from DR. *He does a lap of the stage, then runs out* DL, *waving to the audience, as the Lights fade to Black-out*

Music to cover the scene change

SCENE 3

Robinson's Hut

The same setting as Act II, Scene 1 can be used with the addition of Robinson's hut placed C. *The hut is small and crudely constructed from bamboo with large leaves for a roof. It has a small doorway at the front, covered by a piece of sailcloth. Over the door hangs a piece of driftwood on which is written "Robinson's Rest". The stage is empty*

To suitable music, the Children, as exotic birds, small monkeys and other jungle wildlife, creep on from both sides. They examine the hut with timid curiosity, then perform a dance around it

Song 11

After the dance and applause, Robinson is heard singing inside the hut, refrain of Song 2

On hearing this, the Children scatter in alarm and exit in all directions

Robinson emerges from the hut. He now wears a short costume made from natural materials

Robinson (*seeing the audience; greeting them*) Oh, hi, folks! (*He indicates the hut, proudly*) Well! What do you think? All my own work! Not bad, eh? I knew watching *Changing Rooms* and *Ground Force* would come in handy some day! And what do you think of the gear? (*He indicates the costume and does a twirl*) I found them just lying around. They were probably left over from a—wait for it—*jungle* sale! (*He laughs, then becomes sad*) I wish I knew what happened to Ma and the others. Poor old Ma! (*He takes a large picture from his belt*) I'm glad I've still got this picture of her. (*He shows the picture to the audience*) I think I'll hang it on my hut. It might scare off any wild animals! (*He fixes the picture to the front of the hut*) And what's to become of me? Am I doomed to spend the rest of my life on this desert island! (*He sighs*) And my darling Polly. Will I ever see her again? I miss her so much. (*He sighs*)

Song 12

Sad romantic solo with suitable spot Lighting

Oh, well! I suppose I'll just have to make the best of things and hope that one day a passing ship will rescue me. (*He looks about and shivers*) D'you know, I've still got the feeling I'm being watched. Kids, will you do me a favour? I'm going inside to get some sleep. If you see anyone—or any*thing*, will you give me a shout? You will! Great! Just shout "Robinson" as loud as you can. Thanks.

Robinson yawns and goes into the hut

Slight pause

Friday creeps on from L, *looking towards the hut*

The audience shout "Robinson"

Friday runs off L

Robinson comes out

Yes? Was there someone here?

Act II, Scene 3

"Yes!" from the audience

Well, I can't see anyone!

Robinson yawns and goes into the hut

Friday creeps on from L and approaches the hut

The audience shout "Robinson!" Friday quickly hides behind the hut

Robinson comes out

Yes? Is there someone here?

"Yes!" from the audience

Well, I can't see anyone! Where?

"Behind the hut!" from the audience

Behind the hut? Right! I'll investigate! (*He creeps up the left side of the hut*)

Friday creeps down the right side and cowers at the front of the hut

(*Calling from behind the hut*) There's no-one back here, kids! Where is he now?

"At the front!" from the audience

Robinson creeps down the right side. Friday cowers. Robinson reaches the front, but looks off R, into the wings

Friday seizes the opportunity and dashes off L

Robinson turns and looks at the front of the hut

There's no-one here! I think you lot are having me on! Oh, yes, you are! (*He yawns*) I really must get some sleep!

Robinson goes into the hut

Friday creeps on from L, and goes to the hut

The audience shout "Robinson!" Friday quickly hides behind the hut

Robinson comes out, yawning

Yes? (*He looks about*) Oh, you're at it again! There's no-one here, is there?

"*Yes!*" *from the audience*

Well, where is he?

"*Behind the hut!*"

You'd better be right this time!

Robinson goes up the right side of the hut as Friday comes down the left side. This continues and accelerates until both of them are running around the hut at top speed. Finally Robinson stops at the front and waits. Friday runs slap bang into him. He gives a terrified yell and is about to run away

(*Grabbing his arm*) Wait! Don't run away. There's nothing to be frightened of. I'm not going to hurt you. (*He smiles and gives Friday a friendly pat on the shoulder*)

After a moment of uncertainty, a big grin spreads over Friday's face. He falls to his knees and salaams to Robinson

Hey! There's no need for that! I'm not [local bigwig]! (*He hauls Friday to his feet, then points to himself*) Me—friend—friend.
Friday (*puzzled*) Fred?
Robinson (*laughing*) No, not Fred! Friend!
Friday (*pointing to Robinson*) Fri-fr-friend!
Robinson (*nodding*) That's right! Friend!
Friday (*nodding excitedly*) Friend! Friend! Friend! Friend!
Robinson (*to the audience*) By George, I do believe he's got it! (*He stops Friday*) Wow! All right! (*He points to himself*) My—name—is—Robinson Crusoe. Robin-son Cru-soe.
Friday (*pointing to himself*) Robin-son Cru-soe!
Robinson (*shaking his head*) No. (*He points at himself*) Me Robinson Crusoe!
Friday (*pointing to Robinson*) Me Robinson Crusoe!
Robinson (*laughing*) That's near enough! What—is—*your* (*he points to Friday*) name? *Your* name? (*He points again*)

Puzzled, Friday looks over his shoulder to see what Robinson is pointing at

Friday Goomba?

Act II, Scene 3   53

Robinson (*laughing and turning Friday to face him*) Me Robinson! (*He points to Friday*) You?
Friday (*catching on*) Ah! (*He points to himself, very proudly*) Me—Jajanatumbatanganacombakinteeunga!
Robinson (*gobsmacked*) I... I see! (*To the audience*) Phew! I wonder if that includes his address and post code! (*To Friday*) Well, I don't think I shall ever be able to remember all that. I'll have to find you a shorter name. Something like one of the days of the week, perhaps. Shall I call you Monday? No! Monday's not a very popular day, is it? How about Friday? Everyone likes Friday! Yes, that's it! I'll call you Friday. (*He points to Friday*) You—Friday!
Friday (*pointing to himself*) Me—Friday!
Robinson Well done!
Friday (*nodding excitedly*) Friday! Friday! Fr... (*Suddenly his face clouds over and he shakes his head*) Gumba bonga boo!
Robinson What's wrong?
Friday (*pointing to Robinson*) You Robinson *Crusoe!* Crusoe! Crusoe! (*He points to himself*) Friday! (*He shrugs*)
Robinson Oh, I get it. You want *two* names like me! Now let me think. How about—*good* Friday? *Last* Friday? Friday *week*? No, none of those sound right. (*To the audience*) Have you got any ideas, folks?

The audience call back

Pan Friday? No, I don't think... *Dan* Friday? Oh, *Man* Friday! Yes! That's a good one! (*To Friday*) We'll call you *Man* Friday!
Friday (*pointing to himself*) Man Friday?
Robinson You like it?
Friday (*proudly*) Man Friday! (*He nods*)
Robinson Man Friday and Robinson Crusoe—friends! (*He takes Friday's hand and shakes it*)

Friday is wary at first, then warms to it, and starts shaking Robinson's arm like a pump handle

Friday Friends! Friends! Man Friday—Robinson Crusoe—friends! (*He dances about with glee*)

Song 13

A friendship/partners duet for Robinson and Friday. It starts with Robinson singing most of it while teaching Friday to come in with the odd word. He learns amazingly quickly and soon they are both singing in unison. It ends with a dance routine and singing reprise

After the number, Friday goes up to the hut and points to the picture of Ma

Friday Oomba Jumba?
Robinson *(joining him)* Oh, that's a picture of my mother.
Friday Uh?
Robinson My—mother... *(Not unkindly)* Oh, you wouldn't understand.
Friday *(pointing at the picture)* Ooga! Ooga! *(He gestures, indicating Ma's shape, etc. He then does a good impersonation of her walk and mannerisms)*
Robinson *(laughing)* Yes! That's just like my dear old Ma... *(Suddenly struck)* But how do you know what...?
Friday *(pointing off R)* Zumba! Zumba!
Robinson *(excitedly)* You mean you've *seen* her? You've seen Ma?

Nodding, Friday points to the picture, then off R

(Indicating) Where? Show me! Show me!

Friday goes to the exit R and gestures for Robinson to follow

They exit

The Gorilla lumbers on from L

He sees the hut and goes to explore. The picture of Ma catches his attention and he takes it down. He looks lovingly at it, gives a deep sigh, then plants a noisy kiss on it. He sighs again and holds the picture to his heart, as the Lights fade to Black-out

Music to cover the scene change

SCENE 4

Another Part of the Island

Tabs, or the front cloth used in Act II, Scene 2

The Crimson Hawk enters from DR, still with drawn sword

Hawk *(to the audience)* Ahoy there, shipmates! Have you seen any sign of Ma and Willy?

"No" from the audience

Act II, Scene 4

Neither have I. I've looked everywhere. Let's hope they escaped from the Islanders and are safe in hiding somewhere. *(She re-sheaths her sword and takes the map from her sash)* I'd better continue my search for the treasure. *(She looks at the map)* That temple has got to be somewhere in this area. It's got to be!

The Hawk exits DL

Slight pause

Ma Crusoe creeps on from DR

Looking behind him, Willy creeps on behind her

At C, *Ma stops suddenly and Willy bumps into her. Both yell in fright*

Ma *(to the audience)* Oh, you wouldn't believe the time we've 'ad, folks! Them Islanders chased us all round the island! I never want to go through that again not if I live to be thirty-five! Oh, I wish we'd never found that treasure map! It's been nothin' but trouble! Pirates! Shipwreck! Islanders! What else can happen to us?!

The Gorilla enters from DR

The audience will be shouting out a warning as it creeps up behind them

(To the audience, clinging to Willy) W-what is it? Is there s-someone behind us?
Willy *(to the audience)* Is it the Islanders?
Ma *(to the audience)* Is it the pirates?

"No!" from the audience

Ma⎫
Willy⎭ *(together)* What is it then?!!

"A Gorilla!" etc.

Ma *(to the audience)* A gorgonzola! What rubbish!
Ma⎫
Willy⎭ *(together; to the audience)* Oh, no, there isn't!

Routine with the audience follows. During it, the Gorilla moves down and stands beside Willy

Willy sees it, does a "silent scream", and runs out DR

The Gorilla moves into Willy's position beside Ma

Ma (*oblivious, facing front*) Oh, Willy! Per'aps they're right! Per'aps there is a gorgonzola after all!! (*She gets scared*) 'Old yer poor old Mummy's 'and so she won't be so frightened! (*She holds out her right hand*)

The Gorilla takes it and strokes it gently

That's better. Oh, you are a comfort to me, Willy... I said you——

She looks at the Gorilla and does a huge double take. She yells and tries to run away to L, *but the Gorilla is still holding her hand. He pulls her back and wraps his arms around her*

(*Yelling and struggling*) 'Elp! I've been grabbed by the anthropoids! 'Elp!!

Willy rushes on from DR, *and stands transfixed*

(*To Willy*) Well, don't just stand there! Can't you see I'm bein' monkeyed about with! Do something!!
Willy Like what?
Ma I don't know! Offer it a cup of PG Tips or somethin'!
Gorilla (*grunting at Ma and patting her gently on the head*) Ooo! Ooo! (*He tickles her under the chin*)
Willy (*moving a little closer*) Hey! I think he likes you, Ma!
Ma (*to the audience*) I know I always bring out the beast in men—but *this* is ridiculous!

The Gorilla releases Ma, and produces—from somewhere about its person!— the picture of Ma. He points to it

What's that? David Attenborough's autograph? (*She looks at the picture and reacts*) 'Ere! That's a picture of me!
Willy (*looking*) Crikey! It's the one you gave to Robinson last Christmas!
Ma So it is! (*Excitedly*) That means 'e must be 'ere somewhere! (*To Gorilla*) Come on, Tarzan, tell us where you got that!

The Gorilla kisses the picture. He turns to Ma and advances on her, making kissing noises

(*Backing away* L) Oh, no! Go away! I 'aven't got me kiss-proof lippy on!

Act II, Scene 4   57

Suddenly the sound of distant drum beats is heard. The Gorilla stops to listen with its head cocked

Willy Ma! I can 'ear drums!
Ma Nah! That's just 'is 'eart pounding'. I always 'ave that effect on men—animal or vegetable!

The Gorilla bounds off DR

(*Calling after it*) Oy! Come back! (*She joins Willy* C) Oh, drat! 'E might 'ave been able to take us to Robinson!
Willy Well, at least we know 'e's somewhere on the island. The picture proves it.

Suddenly, the Medicine Man and an Islander leap on from DR

Medicine Man (*yelling*) Tumba Boya!!
Ma Yah! Run for it!

Ma and Willy run to the exit DL

The sudden appearance of another threatening Islander there, halts them in their tracks

Ma and Willy back away C *and huddle together*

Medicine Man (*pointing his skull wand at them*) Zaboota! Kala Boogar! Kala Boogar!
Willy W-wos 'e mean, Ma?
Ma I dunno, but I don't think it's "have a nice day"!
Medicine Man (*to Islanders*) Tumba Boya! Tumba Boya!

The two Islanders grab Ma and Willy and drag them out DL. *The Medicine Man follows*

Robinson enters from DR, *followed by Man Friday*

The drum beats fade out

Robinson Oh, no! This is awful! The Islanders have captured Ma and Willy! What am I going to do?! Friday, where are they taking them?

Friday doesn't understand. Robinson points off L, *and gestures questioningly*

Where—take—Ma and Willy?
Friday (*wide-eyed with awe and dread*) Boogar!
Robinson Boogar? What's ... wait a minute! That rings a bell! Yes! It was on the map! I remember now! The Temple of Boogar!
Friday (*falling to his knees and bowing*) Boogar! Boogar!
Robinson It must be their god. But why would they take Ma and Willy to... (*He hauls Friday to his feet*) Friday! Why—Ma—Willy—Boogar? Why?
Friday Ma— (*he makes a slashing motion across his belly*) Willy— (*he repeats the motion, then raises his hands in awesome reverence*) Boogar!
Robinson (*horrified*) You mean... This is terrible! I've got to save them!
Friday— (*with appropriate gestures*) you—take—Robinson—to—Boogar! Yes?! (*He nods*)

Friday understands, and goes to the exit DL *and gestures for Robinson to follow. They exit*

Villainous music as Blackbeard enters from DR, *dragging Captain Bowsprit* C. *Bessie follows, being pushed on by Patch. She is now bound with ropes*

Blackbeard Ha har! (*He snarls at the audience*) Geraaah!!
Patch (*to the audience*) Ger!
Blackbeard (*to Bessie*) An' now, me pretty! I've got a very special torture—just for you! (*With an evil chuckle*) Hee! Hee!
Bessie (*cowering against her father*) Ooo! Daddy!
Captain Be brave, m'dear! Be brave.
Blackbeard (*to Captain*) You'll soon tell me where the treasure is when you sees what I've got in store fer yer darlin' little girl! Mr Patch!
Patch (*aside to the audience*) 'Ere we go again! (*To Blackbeard*) Ay ay, Cap'n! (*He gingerly takes a cloth bag from the inside pocket of his coat*)
Captain (*scornfully*) Huh! Not those pathetic worms again! My daughter ain't afraid of a few worms! Are you, m'dear?
Bessie (*who obviously is*) N-no, Daddy!
Blackbeard (*with devilish glee*) Oh, it bain't worms *this* time! It be somethin'—*much worse*! Ha har! Show 'em, Mr Patch!

Patch very gingerly opens the bag and peers right inside. Suddenly his head jerks back and the bag seems to take on a life of its own. Comic business as Patch appears to be wrestling with the bag's contents. He is jerked about and thrown to the ground, etc. Eventually, he extracts from the bag a huge, hairy black spider. He lets it "wriggle" about long enough for the others and the audience to see, then he manages to stuff it back into the bag. He is exhausted after his ordeal and stands gripping the neck of the bag, which still gives spasmodic jerks. Bessie is petrified and cowers against her father

Act II, Scene 4   59

Don't ee like spiders, me pretty?

Bessie wails

Ha har! I thought not! Just imagine 'avin' that one *wrigglin'* an' *crawlin'* about in yer 'air!

Bessie wails

Ha har! (*To Captain*) Tell me what I wants to know, or she'll be wearin' the latest thing in tarantula hats!
Bessie Daddy!

The Captain is silent and unshakeable

Blackbeard So be it! (*He roars at Bessie*) Down on yer knees!

Bessie falls to her knees

One last chance, Captain! Where's the treasure?!

The Captain is still unmovable

(*To Patch*) Do it!

Patch holds the bag over Bessie's head and slowly prepares to open it. Bessie is squirming and gibbering with terror

Bessie No! No! (*Pleadingly*) Daddy! Tell him! Please—tell him! Daddy! Pleeeeease!!

This is too much for the Captain and he gives in

Captain Enough! I'll tell you!

With a triumphant bellow of laughter, Blackbeard signals to Patch. He stuffs the bag into his inside pocket. Bessie jumps up and rushes to her father

Blackbeard Now! Where be the treasure?
Captain From what I can remember of the map, it's buried on this side of the island—in an Islander temple. I'd say, somewhere in (*he nods to* L) that direction.
Blackbeard A temple, y'say! That should be easy to find! But I'll be atakin' you along as a guide, Captain! (*He puts the cutlass to Captain's throat*) An'

'eaven help the pair of ee if you'm lyin'! (*To the audience*) Ha har! Soon the treasure will be mine! All mine! Ha har! (*To Captain*) Lead on, Brown Owl! (*He prods the Captain and Bessie with his cutlass*)

They all exit DL, *as the Lights fade to Black-out*

Drum beats to cover the scene change

SCENE 5

The Temple of Boogar

Raised, UC, *is a huge stone idol of the hideous god Boogar. There is a stone altar in front of the idol (see Production Notes). The side wings represent crumbling stone pillars. The backcloth shows a wall of massive stone blocks. Both the wall and pillars are covered with grotesque carvings and partly overgrown with jungle creepers. (Note: if facilities are limited, the same setting as Act II, Scene 1 and 3 can be used with the addition of the idol and the altar) Red torch light effect, casting eerie shadows over the scene*

The Islanders are discovered, engaged in a dance. Alternatively, they can be standing at the sides, chanting as speciality dancer/s perform a dance. Whatever is chosen it must create a sinister and menacing atmosphere

Song 14

After the number, the drum beats continue

The dancer/s, if used, can exit or join the other Islanders

The Medicine Man leaps on from R *to* C

He does a few grotesque gyrations, then kneels US, *facing the idol. All the Islanders do the same. The Medicine Man raises his arms and the drum beats stop*

A pause

Medicine Man (*bowing to the idol*) Kala Boogar!
Islanders (*bowing*) Kala Boogar!

They all stand and the drum beats start again. The Medicine Man points R *with his wand*

Act II, Scene 5   61

Medicine Man Abooga Boya!

Willy and Ma Crusoe are pushed on from R. *They are followed by an Islander who is prodding Ma with his knife*

Ma Ahooow! (*To Islander*) All right! All right! I get the point! (*She rubs her rear*)
Willy (*looking about in awe*) What's this place, Ma?
Ma Well, it ain't the [local pub or night spot], unless they've 'ad it done up!
Willy (*seeing the idol*) Look at that!!
Ma (*looking*) Crikey! What's [local or topical personality] doin' 'ere? That must be their god! Old Boogie Woogie, or whatever 'is name is!
Medicine Man (*pointing at them*) Zaboota!

The Islander pushes Ma and Willy to C, *then joins the other Islanders. The Medicine Man goes to Willy and peers very closely at him*

Willy (*timidly*) H-hullo ... nice year we're 'avin' for the time of weather...

The Medicine Man gives a strange cry and leaps in the air. He dances around Ma and Willy, chanting and waving his wand. Joining in the chant, the Islanders dance on the spot

Ma (*to the audience*) This'd go down a bomb at the [local gag]!

The Medicine Man and Islanders stop dancing. The Medicine Man goes to Ma and peers closely at her

(*To Willy, from the corner of her mouth*) 'Ere, I 'ope 'e doesn't think this is a ladies excuse me!
Medicine Man (*to Ma*) Unga Zaboota! Kala Boogar Boya!
Ma (*to Medicine Man, nodding as if she understood*) Oh, is that right... I 'eard you can get them twenty pence cheaper at [local shop].
Medicine Man (*facing front and yelling a command*) Unga Bunga!!

Unseen by Ma and Willy, an Islander enters from L. *He is carrying a huge, vicious-looking knife*

Willy turns, sees the knife and leaps up into Ma's arms

Willy Ahaaagh!!
Ma (*seeing the knife*) It's all right, Willy. Calm down! (*She lowers him to the ground*) I expect they're gonna cut us a piece of cake!

The Islander crosses to the Medicine Man and hands him the knife

Or per'aps 'e's gonna trim 'is corns!
Medicine Man (*raising the knife in both hands*) Kala Boogar!
Islanders (*raising their knives*) Kala Boogar!
Ma (*raising her hands*) Hallelujah!

With upraised knife, the Medicine Man advances on Ma and Willy. They yell and run away. The Medicine Man chases them around the stage. Suddenly a deep, unearthly roar emulates from the idol itself. It reverberates around the stage. The Lighting becomes dark and the idol and altar are illuminated by an eerie glow. The Medicine Man and the Islanders freeze in terror. The arms of the idol come to life and start waving about. There is another terrifying roar. The Islanders scream and fall to their knees. The Medicine Man drops the knife and runs to cower DR. *Ma and Willy cower* DL

Slowly, the lid of the altar slides open and a ghoulish figure rises from inside. It is clothed in a ragged, hooded garment of greenish grey. One sleeved arm obscures its face

It steps out of the altar, and lowers its arm to expose a hideous skull face

At the sight of this, the Medicine Man and the Islanders scream and run out in all directions

At this point the Lighting becomes brighter, and the eerie glow gradually fades out. The arms of the idol remain still. Ma and Willy are huddled together with their eyes squeezed shut and their knees knocking. The "ghost" moves to behind them. They open their eyes and peer at each side

Willy (*trembling*) Ooo, Ma! H-has it gone?
Ma (*trembling*) I-I don't know! (*To the audience*) Has it gone, kids?

"No!" from the audience

Willy W-where is it, then?

"Behind you!"

Ma and Willy gulp, then turn slowly around. The "ghost" raises its arms and gives a ghoulish howl. Ma and Willy yell and run around the stage in a panic

The "ghost" exits R

Act II, Scene 5 63

Ma and Willy crash into each other, fall to the ground and cover their heads in fear. The voice of Robinson is heard coming from the idol. It sounds normal, but greatly amplified

Robinson (*from the idol*) Yoo hoo! Ma! Willy!

Ma and Willy sit up with a jolt and face front, puzzled

(*From the idol*) Ma! Willy!
Ma Crikey! I'm 'earing voices now!
Willy Same 'ere! An' it sounded like Robinson!
Robinson (*from the idol*) It *is* Robinson! Look behind you!

They swivel around on their bottoms to face the idol. It waves its arms

(*From the idol*) Hallo, Ma! Hallo, Willy!

They jump to their feet and rush up to the idol

Ma Robinson! Is it really you?!
Robinson (*from the idol*) Yes, Ma. It's really me!
Ma (*horrified*) Oh! My poor lamb! What 'ave they done to you! They've turned you into [topical personality]!
Robinson (*laughing*) It's all right. Don't panic. I'll be with you in a moment.

The arms of the idol return to the set position

Robinson emerges from behind the idol, dusting himself off

Here I am!

Ma and Willy rush to greet him

Ma (*hugging him*) Oh, my Robbie!
Willy Y'mean—you were hidin' inside that idol all the time?

Robinson nods

An' it was you who frightened off the Islanders?

Robinson nods

An' to think, Ma, you always called *me* an idle so-an-so!

All three laugh, then Ma is struck by a sobering thought

Ma 'Ere! Just a minute! (*To Robinson*) If *you* were in *there*! (*She points to the idol*) Who—or what—was in *there*? (*She points to the altar*)
Willy Oh, yeah! The ghost!
Robinson What ghost?

The Ghost enters from R

Ma and Willy yell and rush away to L

Ma
Willy } (*together*) That one!!

Laughing, Robinson goes over to the Ghost and puts his hand on its shoulder

Robinson This is no ghost! Look! (*He pushes back the hood and pulls down a skull mask to reveal the beaming face of Man Friday*) This is a new friend I met on the island. His name's Man Friday. (*He leads Friday to* C) Ma, meet Man Friday. Man Friday, meet Ma.

Ma and Willy come over

Ma Charmed ever so!
Friday (*holding out his hand to her*) Friend!

She takes his hand. Comic business as he gives her the pump handle treatment

(*To Willy, holding out his hand*) Friend!
Ma (*aside to Willy*) Brace yerself!

Willy takes Friday's hand. Instead of getting the pump treatment, he gets a polite little shake

(*To the audience*) Well! Would you Adam an' Eve it!
Friday (*urgently pulling Robinson up to the altar*) Oomba Boya! Oomba Boya!
Robinson What's wrong, Friday?
Friday (*pointing to the inside of the altar*) Oomba Boya!
Robinson (*looking inside*) What is it? Hey! There's a box in here!

Ma and Willy rush up to join them

Act II, Scene 5   65

Help me lift it out.

Together they haul out a chest and place it on the ground in front of the altar

Ma Are you thinkin' what I'm thinkin'?
Robinson The treasure?! It's got to be!
Ma Well, don't just stand there—open the box!

Robinson kneels in front of the chest. He hesitates, then opens the lid. They all gasp as the glittering wealth is revealed. Gold bars and goblets, sparkling jewels, strings of pearls, heaps of gold coins, etc. Robinson lifts up objects and lets the coins run through his fingers

Robinson (*in wondrous disbelief*) We've found it! We've actually found Flint's treasure!

With yells of delight, Ma and Willy dance for joy

   Suddenly, Blackbeard strides on from L. *Bessie and Captain Bowsprit follow with Patch bringing up the rear*

Blackbeard (*waving his cutlass*) Ha har!

All merriment stops dead. Robinson stands up

Ma Oh, no! It's the blackpuddin'!

Ma, Willy and Friday clear to R. *Robinson remains in front of the chest*

Blackbeard So, Robinson Crusoe, you've found my treasure for me! I'm much obliged to ee! T'will save me the trouble of 'avin' to dig it up!
Robinson (*hands on hips, defiantly*) This is not *your* treasure, Blackbeard! It's *our* treasure!
Blackbeard (*snarling*) We'll see about that, ya swab! 'And it over! 'And it over, or I'll... (*He puts the cutlass to Bessie's throat*) Slit their gizzards!!

Bessie screams. Robinson is forced to give in

Robinson Very well. You win. Take the treasure—but let them go free.

Bessie and the Captain are released and they run cross to Ma and the others. Their bonds are removed. Robinson joins them. Blackbeard and Patch rush to the chest and gloat over the treasure

Blackbeard Ha har! 'Tis mine at last! (*To the audience*) I told ee I'd get it, you scurvy landlubbers! Ha har! (*He shuts the lid*)

Blackbeard and Patch lift the chest, and proceed to carry it towards the exit L

Suddenly, the Crimson Hawk enters from there with a drawn sword

This causes the two pirates to halt in their tracks

Hawk (*striking a pose*) Avast there, Blackbeard!
Blackbeard You!!
Hawk Yes! 'Tis I, the Crimson Hawk! I've come to claim that treasure!
Blackbeard (*with a mocking laugh*) Ho! Ho! Ho! Well, you'm too late, Missy! 'Tis all mine!
Hawk Why don't we settle this matter in the traditional pirate fashion? Let us fight for it. Just you and I. Winner takes all.
Blackbeard (*scornfully*) *Me* fight with *you*!
Hawk Not afraid, are you, Blackbeard?
Blackbeard (*enraged*) Afraid! The mighty Blackbeard afraid of a flimsy female! (*He brandishes his cutlass*) I'll rip ee apart in 'alf a second!
Hawk You're welcome to try! (*She adopts a stance*) On guard!

Hawk and Blackbeard commence to fight. The fight is accompanied by suitable "fight" music. The duel should be as elaborate and spectacular as possible, making use of the whole stage and a follow spot. Hawk is a nimble, expert swordswoman. Blackbeard obviously went to the "cut and thrust" school! Finally, Blackbeard is disarmed and forced to his knees by Hawk's sword point, C. *The music and the spotlight fade out. Ma and the others cheer. Patch tries to hide behind the treasure chest*

So, Blackbeard! What do you say now? Not bad for a "flimsy female", eh?

Blackbeard just growls. Robinson and Willy drag Patch out from behind the chest and force him to his knees beside Blackbeard. Ma jeers and pokes her tongue out at them

Willy (*to the audience*) What shall we do with them, folks? Got any ideas?

The audience are sure to have several

Ma (*to Hawk*) Go on, girl! Give 'im a dose of 'is own medicine! Slit 'is blizzard—or whatever it's called!
Hawk No, that is not my way. No unnecessary killing. He's been defeated, that's good enough for me. Blackbeard, you and your companion will be

Act II, Scene 5

marooned on this desert island. Let us hope that the civilized world never has to set eyes on you again.

The others agree

(*Prodding Blackbeard with the sword point*) Now go! Take your ugly face away from here!

Amid boos and hisses, Blackbeard and Patch get to their feet and slouch to the exit L. *Blackbeard turns for a final snarl at the others and the audience*

Patch It could be worse, Cap'n.
Blackbeard How?!
Patch We could be marooned in [local place]!

With a bellow of rage, Blackbeard chases Patch out L

Hawk puts away her sword

Ma Thank goodness for that. That's the last time we'll see 'is furry fizzog!
Robinson I wouldn't be too sure of that, Ma. Don't forget—*we're* marooned on the island as well.
Hawk Ah, but you're *not*! My ship is at your disposal. I shall be more than happy to return you all safely to England!

The others are overjoyed and express their thanks

Ma (*to the others*) Well, it's the least she could do after swipin' the treasure!
Hawk Ah, yes, the treasure. It really does belong to me, you know. Let me explain. Captain Flint, the notorious pirate who accumulated it in the first place, was my great grandfather. I will not excuse or condone his methods of acquiring it, but acquire it he did and it was considered *his* property. As his only living descendent, I lay claim to the treasure as my rightful inheritance.

Murmurs of agreement from the others

Robinson I see. Well, in that case—it is yours by right.
Hawk Thank you.

Slight pause

Of course—I shall be very happy to share it with you.

Exclamations from the others

Robinson Why?
Hawk Because... (*With a flourish, she removes her hat, bandana and mask to reveal—Polly Perkins*)

The others are totally gobsmacked, not least Robinson

Others Polly Perkins!!
Robinson Polly! I-I don't understand...
Polly (*in her normal voice*) Since I came to your town I have been leading a double life. Polly Perkins, barmaid at the *Sea Dog Inn*, and—the Crimson Hawk, buccaneer extraordinaire! I decided that the only way to find my great-grandfather's treasure was to become a pirate like him. It's in the blood, I suppose.
Robinson And all those times you were supposed to be visiting your sick granny—you were really sailing the high seas as a pirate?
Polly I'm afraid so, Robbie. Please forgive me. Deceiving you was my only regret. But now that the treasure has been found, my pirate days are over. (*She moves to him*) I'm all yours—if you'll have me.
Robinson Oh, Polly!

They embrace

Bessie (*all soppy*) Oh, it's just like [soap opera]!
Ma (*to the audience*) And just about as far-fetched!
Robinson (*to all*) Well! Everything has turned out fine. Polly's found her treasure and I've found mine! As soon as we return home we shall be married!
Others Hurray!
Ma (*aside to Robinson*) That's m'boy! Keep it in the family!
Robinson Friday! (*He brings him forward*) I want you to be best man at my wedding! *Best* Man Friday!
Friday (*nodding and grinning*) *Best* Man Friday!
Willy (*to him, being all soppy with Bessie*) And at our wedding too!
Friday Best Man Friday! Best Man Friday!

Comic business as Friday shakes hands with everyone

Ma (*getting weepy and moving away to* R) Oh, all this talk of weddin's! I wish there was someone to sweep *me* off me feet an' carry me up the aisle!

The Gorilla enters behind her. He can either lift Ma up in his arms, or beat his chest and grunt loudly

Oh, no! I'm not that desperate!

The Gorilla runs off R, *as Ma runs back to the others—straight into the arms of Captain Bowsprit*

Oh! Hallo, sailor! 'Ere! Now that I'm filthy rich, how about you an' me getting better acquainted?
Captain That would give me enormous treasure... I mean—*pleasure.*
Ma Huh! I think you were right the first time!

The music starts and they all go into a joyful song and dance

The Islanders and the Gorilla come on at the back to join in the fun

End with tableau

Song 15 (optional)

After the number, a front cloth is lowered or tabs close

Scene 6

Before the Voyage Home

Tabs, or front cloth used in Act II, Scenes 2 and 4

Willy enters from DR, *waving to the audience*

Willy Hallo, folks! Hey, kids! I've just come to tell you that your suffering is nearly over! Did you enjoy it? Why? What were you doing? You've been a smashin' audience. So good, in fact, you ought to give yourselves a big round of applause! (*He indicates one side*) *This* side first! Turn to *that* side and give 'em a nice big clap!

They do so

Good! Now, *this* side return the compliment!

They do so

Well done! Now all together!

Ma Crusoe bounces on in the midst of applause and thinks it's for her

She curtsies and blows kisses like a prima donna

Ma (*gushing*) Thank you! Thank you! So kind! So kind!
Willy Oy! They weren't clapping you, Ma. They were clapping each other.
Ma (*to the audience*) Clappin' each other! There's a law against that, y'know!

Note: a raffle or some other routine can be substituted for the following

(*To Willy*) Have you told them yet?
Willy No, I was just...
Ma (*pushing him aside*) Then *I'll* do it! (*To the audience*) Ladles and jellyspoons! Tonight we have a really special treat for you!
Willy (*to the audience, á la TV game show*) Ooow!
Ma Tonight we are giving away a fabulous prize!
Willy (*as before*) Ooow!
Ma It's a fortnight's holiday for two in—the Caribbean!!
Willy (*as before*) Ooow!
Ma Underneath one of your seats is a special red dot. Whoever is sitting in the seat with the red dot wins this fabulous holiday! Can we have some lights, please.

The House Lights come up

Now, if you'll all stand up and inspect your seats!

Ad lib as the audience look under their seats. It transpires that all the seats have red dots under them

Ma ⎫
Willy ⎭ (*together, ad lib*) What! *All* of them?! (*Etc., etc.*)
Ma Oh, no! This is awful! Someone's messed things up! I'm very sorry, ladies and gentlemen. You'd better all sit down again!

The House Lights go down

(*Yelling into the wings*) Someone's 'ead will roll for this! (*To the audience*) You just can't get the staff these days!
Willy What are we gonna do now, Ma? They're ever so disappointed.
Ma Yes. We'll have to try and make amends.
Willy (*dumbly*) A men's *what*?
Ma Stupid boy! I know! We'll give them a chance to sing! (*To the audience*) You'll enjoy that, won't you? Oh, yes, you will!

Act II, Scene 7

The song sheet is lowered, or can be brought from the wings by Willy, assisted by the Gorilla or Friday

Song 16

They have fun getting the audience to sing along. Children can be brought on if desired and given sweets. Finally, the song sheet is removed

> *Ma and Willy exit, waving goodbye to the audience, as the Lights fade to Black-out*

SCENE 7

A fanfare

This can be a special Finale setting or one of the previous full stage scenes can be used. Bright Lighting and bouncy music

All enter for the Finale walk down. The last to enter are Robinson and Polly

Robinson And so, dear friends, our tale is told.
Polly We hope it gave you pleasure.
Ma I'm gonna marry my Captain bold.
Captain She really is a treasure.
Bessie As Willy's wife I'll tend his needs.
Willy And I've got quite a few!
Blackbeard I'll soon be back at my pirate deeds!
Patch And we know what they think of you!
Friday We hope you have enjoyed the play,
If you wish to clap, please do so.
There's only one thing left to say——
All (*waving*) Goodbye from Robinson Crusoe!

Finale Song 17 or Reprise

CURTAIN

FURNITURE AND PROPERTY LIST

Further dressing may be added at the director's discretion

ACT I

SCENE 1

On stage: Harbour backcloth
Quayside wings
Inn piece with "Sea Dog" sign board
Ship cut-out with gangplank
Harbour wall
Table
Stools
Barrels
Boxes

Off stage: Cleaning rag (**Polly**)
Letter (**Robinson**)
Sea chest. *In it*: various comic objects, treasure map (**Robinson**)
Bucket, spade (**Bessie**)
Life jacket, water wings (**Ma**)
Kit bag (**Robinson**)

Personal: **Blackbeard**: hat, dagger (throughout)
Patch: eye patch (throughout)
Polly: cloak, bundle
Ma: water wings, life belts

SCENE 2

On stage: Tabs or frontcloth

SCENE 3

On stage: Sky backcloth
Ship's bulwarks

Furniture and Property List

Ship's wings
Life belt
Barrels
Boxes
Telescope on barrel

Off stage: Pirate ship cut-out with Jolly Roger flag (**SM**)

Personal: **Pirates**: cutlasses, pistols
Hawk: hat, bandanna, mask, sword (throughout)
Captain: map

SCENE 4

On stage: Tabs or frontcloth
"Bath tub" cut-out with mast and bloomer sail
"Wave" ground row

Off stage: Shark fin (**SM**)
Toilet brush (**Ma**)
Fly swatter (**Willy**)
Tennis racket (**Bessie**)

SCENE 5

On stage: Undersea backcloth
Undersea wings and ground row
Shell throne
Neptune's trident

Off stage: Sea serpent (**Chorus** or **SM**)

Personal: **Neptune**: large handkerchief

ACT II

SCENE 1

On stage: Island backcloth
Island wings and ground row
Large rock

Off stage: Knives (**Islanders**)
Trick banana (**Gorilla**)

Personal: **Medicine Man:** skull wand (throughout)
Blackbeard: huge cutlass (throughout)
Captain: ropes
Ma: "seaweed" on costume
Hawk: pistol, map, sash

SCENE 2

On stage: Tabs or frontcloth

Personal: **Patch:** bag of edible "worms"
Gorilla: number

SCENE 3

On stage: As Act II, Scene 1, without rock
Robinson's hut. *On it:* sign reading "Robinson's Rest"

Personal: **Robinson:** picture of **Ma**

SCENE 4

On stage: Tabs or frontcloth used in Act II, Scene 2

Personal: **Hawk:** map
Gorilla: picture of **Ma**
Patch: bag containing big hairy "spider"
Bessie: ropes

SCENE 5

On stage: Huge stone idol
Stone altar. *In it:* treasure chest containing gold bars, goblets, jewels, gold coins, etc.
Same setting as Act II, Scenes 1 and 3 can be used, or——
Temple backcloth
Temple wings

Off stage: Huge knife (**Islander**)

Personal: **Friday:** skull, mask, robe
Bessie: bonds
Captain: bonds

Furniture and Property List

SCENE 6

On stage: Tabs or frontcloth used in Act II, Scenes 2 and 4

Off stage: Song sheet (**SM**)
Sweets for children from audience (**Ma** and **Willy**)

SCENE 7

On stage: Finale. Act II, Scene 5 setting can be used, without idol and altar

LIGHTING PLOT

Property fittings required: nil
Various interior and exterior settings

ACT I, SCENE 1

To open:	General exterior lighting	
Cue 1	**Robinson** and **Polly** sing Song 2 *Romantic lighting with follow spot*	(Page 4)
Cue 2	End of Song 2 *Take out spot, return to previous lighting*	(Page 4)
Cue 3	**All** are waving and cheering goodbye *Fade lights to black-out*	(Page 19)

ACT I, SCENE 2

To open:	Gloomy interior lighting	
Cue 4	**Ma** enters *Brighten general lighting*	(Page 20)
Cue 5	**Willy** and **Bessie** exit *Fade lights to black-out*	(Page 23)

ACT I, SCENE 3

To open:	Bright exterior lighting	
Cue 6	**Ma**: "Music!" *Special lighting for Song 6*	(Page 25)
Cue 7	End of Song 6 *Return to previous lighting*	(Page 25)

Lighting Plot

Cue 8	**Blackbeard**: (*off*) "...You'll soon find out!" *Bright flash from off* L	(Page 30)
Cue 9	**Captain** and **Robinson** rush to look off L *Flickering flames effect off* L	(Page 30)
Cue 10	**Captain**: "Abandon ship!!" *Flash of an explosion off* L*; fill whole stage with red, flickering fire effects and lightning flashes; when pandemonium is at its height, black-out*	(Page 31)

ACT I, SCENE 4

To open:	General exterior lighting	
Cue 11	Shark fin appears *Follow spot on shark fin*	(Page 32)
Cue 12	Shark fin goes off *Take out follow spot*	(Page 33)
Cue 13	Shark fin appears *Follow spot on shark fin; repeat follow spot during routine, until final exit of shark fin*	(Page 33)
Cue 14	**All**: "Help!!" *Snap black-out*	(Page 34)

ACT I, SCENE 5

To open:	Special undersea lighting	
Cue 15	**Sea Serpent** enters *Follow spot on* **Robinson** *for his final speech and during the grand tableau*	(Page 37)

ACT II, SCENE 1

To open:	General tropical exterior lighting with dappled sunlight

Cue 16	**Gorilla** exits *Fade lights to black-out*	(Page 45)

ACT II, SCENE 2

To open:	Shady, tropical exterior lighting	
Cue 17	**Gorilla** runs off, waving *Fade lights to black-out*	(Page 49)

ACT II, SCENE 3

To open:	General tropical exterior lighting	
Cue 18	**Wildlife** enter *Special lighting for Song 11*	(Page 49)
Cue 19	End of Song 11 *Return to previous lighting*	(Page 49)
Cue 20	**Robinson** sings Song 12 *Dim out general lighting, bring up spot on* **Robinson**	(Page 50)
Cue 21	End of Song 12 *Take out spot, return to previous lighting*	(Page 50)
Cue 22	**Robinson** and **Friday** sing Song 13 *Follow spot*	(Page 53)
Cue 23	End of Song 13 *Take out follow spot*	(Page 53)
Cue 24	**Gorilla** holds picture to his heart *Fade lights to black-out*	(Page 54)

ACT II, SCENE 4

To open:	Shady, tropical exterior lighting	
Cue 25	**All** exit *Fade lights to black-out*	(Page 60)

Lighting Plot   79

ACT II, SCENE 5

To open: Sinister, red torch light effect, casting eerie shadows

Cue 26   The idol roars   (Page 62)
           Fade stage lights and bring up eerie glow on idol and
           altar

Cue 27   **Medicine Man** and **Islanders** run off   (Page 62)
           Gradually bring up brighter general lighting, fading
           out eerie glow and torchlight effect

Cue 28   **Hawk** and **Blackbeard** fence   (Page 66)
           Follow spot

Cue 29   **Blackbeard** falls to his knees   (Page 66)
           Take out follow spot

ACT II, SCENE 6

To open: Overall general lighting

Cue 30   **Ma**: "Can we have some lights, please."   (Page 70)
           Bring up house lights

Cue 31   **Ma**: "You'd better all sit down again!"   (Page 70)
           Fade house lights

Cue 32   **Ma** and **Willy** exit   (Page 71)
           Fade lights to black-out

ACT II, SCENE 7

To open: Bright lighting

No cues

EFFECTS PLOT

ACT I

Cue 1   **Patch** exits   (Page 17)
2 loud splashes off L

Cue 2   Song 6   (Page 25)
Taped music for dance (optional)

Cue 3   Bright flash from off L   (Page 30)
Loud explosion off L

Cue 4   **Captain** and **Robinson** rush to look off L   (Page 30)
Cloud of smoke from off L

Cue 5   **Captain**: "Abandon ship!!"   (Page 31)
Explosion; fill whole stage with smoke; sounds of whistles, wind, crashing waves and thunder

Cue 6   Black-out   (Page 31)
Cut all effects

Cue 7   During black-out   (Page 34)
Sound effect of water gurgling down plug hole

Cue 8   To open Scene 5   (Page 34)
Undersea sounds

ACT II

Cue 9   To open Scene 1   (Page 38)
Tropical birdsong and monkey chatter

Cue 10   **Gorilla** unzips banana   (Page 38)
Distant jungle drum beats, gradually getting nearer

Effects Plot

Cue 11	**Gorilla** exits *Drum beats grow louder*	(Page 38)
Cue 12	**Medicine Man** raises his arms *Cut drum beats*	(Page 39)
Cue 13	**Ma**: "I 'aven't got me kiss-proof lippy on!" *Distant drum beats*	(Page 56)
Cue 14	**Robinson** and **Friday** enter *Fade out drum beats*	(Page 57)
Cue 15	**All** exit *Drum beats to cover scene change, and continue into next scene for dance routine and beyond*	(Page 60)
Cue 16	**Medicine Man** raises his arms *Cut drum beats*	(Page 60)
Cue 17	**All** stand *Drum beats*	(Page 60)
Cue 18	**Medicine Man** chases **Ma** and **Willy** *Loud, inhuman roar from idol*	(Page 62)
Cue 19	Arms of idol wave about *Another roar from idol*	(Page 62)
Cue 20	**Hawk**: "On guard!" *Taped "fight" music for fencing duel (optional)*	(Page 66)
Cue 21	**Blackbeard** falls to his knees *Fade out taped music (optional)*	(Page 66)

www.ingramcontent.com/pod-product-compliance
Ingram Content Group UK Ltd.
Pitfield, Milton Keynes, MK11 3LW, UK
UKHW021844210426
5322IPUK00022B/454